FUMES *and a* PRAYER

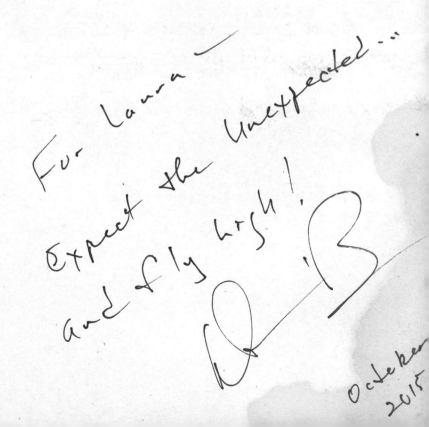

For Laura —
Expect the Unexpected...
and fly high!

October
2015

FUMES *and a*
PRAYER

HOW TO LIVE AT THE EDGE
and STILL BE HOME FOR DINNER

DENNIS BAUER

Fumes and a Prayer:
How to Live at the Edge and Still Be Home for Dinner
by Dennis Bauer

For more information, for copies of this book, and to book Dennis Bauer for speaking engagements, visit www.DennisBauer.com or email Dennis@DennisBauer.com.

First Printing 2011
Printed in the United States of America
ISBN 9780615439426

To everyone who ever got to a gas station

on fumes and a prayer

NOTE TO EVERYONE:

This is a true story. Certain names, places and brands are mentioned; however no endorsement is intended or implied of any service, airport, aircraft or anything else the reader might seek an endorsement of, specifically or in general. Though it's a true story, the story is used anecdotally to illustrate principles the reader may find valuable in life.

NOTE TO THE AVIATION WORLD:

This book is written with the general public in mind and explanations of avionics and aeronautics have been simplified for the non-pilot. If you are a pilot, feel free to mentally add all the technicalities and details you need in order to have a satisfactory picture in your own mind.

NOTE TO THE NON-AVIATION WORLD:

This book is not a treatise or instruction manual on flying. If you want to learn to fly, go to your local airport and learn from a reputable flying school.

CONTENTS

ACKNOWLEDGEMENTS

Heather, Erin and Dennis, Jr., my kids, who made my life as a dad very rich, and who listened to my stories at the dinner table.

Darren LaCroix, 2001 Toastmasters World Champion of Public Speaking, who told me once that this should be my story.

Sybrian Castleman, Vic Everett, Melissa Jurcan, Wayne Osborn, Rebecca Reece, and Greta Hewitt who proofread and offered insights.

Cessna Aircraft Company, who gave permission to use the photo of the Stationair on the cover.

David Anderson, my friend at Bill's Boathouse, who gave me the beautiful, lakeside space for writing, and for being a wild man!

Sarah Zarelli, my step daughter-in-law, for the use of her study while being entertained by the two grandsprouts.

FUMES *and a*
PRAYER

INTRODUCTION

in·tro·duc·tion *noun* \,in-trə-'dək-shən\

to lead inside

FUMES *and a* PRAYER

INTRODUCTION

Flying an airplane involves a journey. Even a short jaunt "around the peapatch" starts somewhere, goes somewhere and ends somewhere. Most flights involve planning a route, and all of them require some understanding of how to make the machine work—how to check systems in the pre-flight inspection, how to take off and climb to altitude, how to maneuver in flight, how to communicate on the radio, how to correct for crosswinds, how to read charts (maps), how to aim for a landing spot and bring the craft back down safely.

The analogy to ventures, relationships and business is easy to make. All involve systems, operations, planning, navigation and communication. Equally important, everyone involved has hopes of a successful journey, no matter how risky, that ends with a safe and smooth landing—their objective reached.

ABOUT ADVENTURES

Most people are risk takers to some extent. There is a spectrum. On one end are those who seek to climb all the tallest peaks of every continent by routes no one has ever taken, bungee jumpers who dive from the tallest bridges, divers who play uncaged with sharks. On the other end are those who take a Sunday drive to somewhere they've never been before—people for whom anything unfamiliar requires courage.

FUMES *and a* PRAYER

Like James Thurber's Walter Mitty, whose larger-than-life, heroic adventures were limited solely to his daydreams, I imagine myself in the untamed corners of the world, facing elements of nature few have ever braved. I am Indiana Jones in the jungles of South America. I am Jacques Cousteau in the depths of the Marianna Trench. I am Jim Whittaker, first American on top of Mount Everest. But these are adventures I will never have outside my own imagination. Perhaps that's true for you too.

I climbed mountains. I flew airplanes and became a flight instructor, and I intend to build my own airplane. I crewed and helmed sailboats. I owned three businesses. I've given many speeches in public—the number one fear of most people, it's said.

I stood on top of 14,410-foot Mount Rainier in late May facing sixty-mile-an-hour winds. I helped crew a forty-foot sailboat during an electrical storm across Puget Sound from Quartermaster Harbor on Vashon Island to Tacoma's Commencement Bay. (The rumor was that lightning doesn't hit boats. But out in open water, that forty-foot aluminum mast looked an awful lot like a lightning magnet with a flashing sign saying, "Hit me! Hit me!")

All that to say: Someone once laughed when I said I didn't want to go with them on a whitewater expedition, shooting rapids down some bucking torrent of wild river. "I don't like to do dangerous things," I replied.

"But you fly airplanes, you climb mountains..." said the Laugher. And, in truth, I *would* attempt Everest—you know, if I were younger, if I had fifty thousand (or so) dollars, if I were in great shape, if I had more experience, if I had a spare two or three months, if I...

I explained to the Laugher: I like adventures; I like danger; I take risks. But they are calculated risks. For years I've said, "I love

INTRODUCTION

adventures, but I always want to be home for dinner." I do like to go to the edge, but I don't want to live there, and I certainly don't want to fall over it. I want to see the edge, climb around on it, fly over it, taste fear, enjoy victory, say I've been there—and later tell others what it was like as we sit around the dinner table.

This book is written for you who are adventurers, people who I think represent the majority of us who take risks, but who don't go over the edge. You want to see the edge; you want to taste the fear; you want to accept the risk; you want to take the challenge. Then, like me, tell everyone about it at the dinner table.

The risks you take might not be outdoor ventures, but they involve no less risk. Certainly relationships are risky; business ventures can make your palms sweaty. For some, standing in front of people to give a speech requires the same pluck as if you ran out the door with a sword to slay a mighty fire-breathing dragon! The challenge is just as fearsome.

THREE WORDS

This book is for you who try anyway. This is not written for those who play it safe to the point of never trying anything. For you who venture out, who try to accomplish anything from the tiniest daydream to the grandest of adventures, three simple words promise guidance for your preparation and for your journey. These three principles work on any scale, from the short seconds of an emergency to the years of business planning and operation. Use these three words to give yourself the best chance of survival and success as you plan ahead in your venture.

FUMES *and a* PRAYER

The same three words, understood before The Unexpected happens, offer the best hope of protecting your progress, of limiting damage and of getting back on course. The three principles in this book will give you the right steps and in the right order to react correctly and confidently to crises when they challenge your resources, your livelihood, your safety or your confidence.

I highly recommend committing the three words to memory. Repeat them, apply them to all situations, practice them so the principles become automatic. Some day you may need to apply them in an instant or two. Always, you can apply what you learn here to your business, to your relationships and to any venture you tackle.

Logbook pages follow each chapter. Use them to jot your notes, ideas, plans and insights that come to mind as you read that chapter.

Buckle up for the journey. I hope you enjoy the ride.

AVIATE • NAVIGATE • COMMUNICATE

INTRODUCTION

FUMES *and a* PRAYER

CHAPTER ONE

FUMES AND A PRAYER

fumes *noun* \'fyümz\ vapors

prayer *noun* \'prer\ a request to God

FUMES *and a* PRAYER

FUMES AND A PRAYER

It was early on a gusty August afternoon as we prepared to take off on the second leg of our flight from Tacoma, Washington, where I lived, to Arapahoe County Airport (now called Centennial Airport) just south of Denver. The high-wing Cessna sat on the tarmac at Mountain Home, Idaho, quiet and still, like an eagle in a nest with all its energy at rest but ready to rise in an instant. We readied the plane for its flight. Before takeoff, I checked the weather for the route over southern Idaho, Wyoming and northern Colorado. I checked the speed and direction of the winds aloft, especially at the altitude where I would be flying, and even though the skies were mostly clear, I filed an instrument flight plan so I could be in radio contact first with Salt Lake Center and then Denver Center all the way from the Mountain Home airport to the Denver area. It was a beautiful afternoon. It would be smooth sailing for sure!

Three passengers and I climbed into the cabin of the clean, white airplane with its large registration number painted on the side, called the "N-number", N1065V. A pilot would read that as "November-One-Zero-Six-Five-Victor," often shortened to the last three characters. Six-Five-Victor seats five passengers plus a pilot, has ample luggage space, and is considered a work horse of an airplane, especially with its turbo-charged engine.

Two passengers climbed aboard through the double side doors on the right side of the plane; one took a seat in the back row, the other in the middle row. The third passenger stepped up onto the footstep attached to the landing strut and sat in the front right seat. I took my place in the front left seat, typically where the "pilot-in-command" sits. I was the only pilot aboard that day.

All passengers received a reminder about fastening their seatbelts securely and about the use of the oxygen masks should we need them. I organized my charts, maps of the airways I planned to follow, along with radio frequencies and airport information I would need. The pre-flight checklist complete, I went through the engine start-up procedures, again following a checklist. Electrical power was turned on; you could hear the hum of the airplane coming alive, alert for the jump into the skies. The propeller area was cleared to start, and the engine sprang to life with gusto, a rich, throaty roar. The propeller beat the air, ready for action.

I set the navigation and communication radios and contacted the tower for clearance to taxi to the runway. Then, cleared for takeoff by the Mountain Home tower, I pointed the nose of the airplane straight down Runway One-Two toward the southeast. I pushed the throttle fully forward, and the powerful, 300 horse-power engine exerted its full strength, charging ahead to lift the thirty-six hundred pounds of aircraft, fuel, passengers and baggage into the sky. We climbed under clear blue skies to the altitude assigned by Salt Lake Center and headed toward Denver, about six hundred nautical miles away.

The normal range of a Cessna Turbo 206F is around six hundred nautical miles, but I planned to fly at a reduced, long-range power setting, and for part of the flight I had a good tailwind. My planning allowed for a reserve of fuel by the time we arrived at Arapahoe County Airport.

Somewhere over mid-Wyoming my radio headset squawked, and Salt Lake Center passed me off to Denver Center. Flying at eleven thousand feet above sea level put us about five thousand feet above the ground. I looked at my three passengers—a slightly built man in his thirties sat on my right; his wife napped in the right seat of the middle two seats, and a young man in his twenties in the back watched lazily as the ground slid slowly by below us.

This airplane has two fuel tanks, one in each wing. A pilot manages the fuel flow to the engine in three ways: paying attention to fuel quantity as indicated on the fuel gauges (one gauge for each tank), switching back and forth between the two fuel tanks with a control lever located on the floor below the instrument panel, and adjusting the fuel/air mixture with a control knob located next to the throttle at the mid-bottom of the instrument panel.

We crossed the border from Wyoming into Colorado. A concern in my mind began to push its way forward so that a mental alarm bell began to say, "Pay attention to me!" I watched the needle on each of the two fuel gauges. They edged closer and closer to the empty mark. This shouldn't be happening! A pilot knows that the best fuel gauge is not the one on the instrument panel anyway; the best gauge is the clock because at a given set of ratios for altitude and engine rpm's, the amount of fuel flowing to the engine is predictable. At a certain rate of fuel flow, the pilot knows how much time he has for the fuel he started with.

I had filled both fuel tanks at Mountain Home. With the predicted tailwinds aloft which I obtained from a current weather briefing, I knew when I took off what my groundspeed should be, how far I could fly, and most importantly, that I had enough fuel to make it to Arapahoe County Airport with plenty to spare. Yet, here were these two fuel gauges telling me that something was wrong.

The clock said I had fuel left. Apparently the gauges didn't know that, because they said that very little fuel remained. My passengers, unaware of the intricacies of fuel management in flight, continued to nap, to read and to watch the ground flow by below. I was not so relaxed.

There's a saying in aviation circles. "Flying is ninety-nine percent pure boredom. The other one percent is pure terror." If you had been there that day, relaxed in one of the passenger seats, you would have heard the constant drone of the engine minute after minute after minute after minute. Somewhere in the vicinity of Fort Collins, taking fuel from the tank in the left wing, The Unexpected happened. You would have heard the engine cough and sputter, and you would have seen the propeller begin to windmill as we coasted through the air.

We were now flying on fumes and a prayer.

Logbook

FUMES *and a* PRAYER

CHAPTER TWO

THE UNEXPECTED

un·ex·pect·ed *adj* \,ən-ik-'spek-təd\

that which hits you from your blindside

FUMES *and a* PRAYER

At the La Grande/Union County Airport, four miles southeast of La Grande, Oregon, it is Saturday morning. The rain stopped, but the skies are gray and the runway is still wet. I have recorded in my flight logbook just seven hours of flight instruction. My instructor, sitting in the right seat of the Cessna 152, a common airplane in which to learn to fly, has had me flying the pattern this morning doing "touch and goes"—take off, fly around the airport, approach to land, reduce power, extend flaps, land but do not stop, flaps up, apply full power, take off again ... and repeat ... and repeat.

Now, sitting on the taxiway with the engine running at idle, touch and goes completed, my instructor asks to see my FAA medical certificate, which also functions as a student pilot permit. I take it out of my wallet, hand it to him and watch him flip to the back side. My heart starts to beat faster as I realize what he is doing. On the back of the medical certificate is a place for the flight instructor to "sign off" the student pilot for solo flight. He takes out his pen, signs his name on my certificate, opens his door, turns to me and shouts over the engine noise, "Congratulations! Go do three touch and goes." He saunters around the back of the plane and heads for the flight office.

I am alone in the cockpit of a flying machine that will be, for the first time, completely under my control, and for which I will be

19

completely responsible—every control, every knob and switch and dial—I am about to become a pilot! Alright ... still a student pilot, technically ... but there is something about that first solo flight that sets you apart, at least in your own mind, from those souls held to the ground by that gentle, unseen and unrelenting force called gravity. I am about to join the few—those few who "flee the surly bonds of earth."

And I've only had seven hours of instruction!

Later, as a flight instructor myself, I would never sign off a student pilot for solo flight until they had at least twice that many hours, and usually closer to three times that many hours of instruction and practice with me sitting in the right seat as their flight instructor and pilot-in-command. Looking back, I cannot believe my instructor signed me off after just seven hours of instruction. I was not a prodigy as a student pilot. Far from it. My white knuckles gripping the control yoke whenever we encountered the slightest turbulence bore witness that I was quite ordinary.

This first solo flight has me at least mildly terrified. I am not ready ... and at the same time, I *am* ready. Has that ever happened to you? Have you ever faced a challenge that you wanted to accept, that charged you up with anticipation? And, at the same time, your heart raced, your senses were on hyper-alert, and you feared failure ... or worse? Yet you stepped out, climbed into the ring, entered the arena, ran onto the field, and you went ahead to accept the challenge?

Taxiing onto Runway Three-Zero, with no control tower at the airport, I click the microphone button to notify any other airplanes in the area that I, solo pilot-to-be, am taking off. "La Grande Traffic, Cessna 92582 ... taking off Runway Three-Zero ... will be in left pattern for touch-and-goes." I release the microphone switch, secure the microphone in its clip, scan the instrument panel and check for any airplanes that might be coming in for a landing. There being none I line up the nose of the airplane with the white centerline running down the length of the runway, snug the seat belt, take a breath, push the throttle full forward for full power and release the brakes.

As the aircraft begins to roll, I have never been so alert in my life. There is no question I can do this ... I've done it a number of times before with the instructor. What scares me is not what I already know. What scares me is—The Unexpected.

Flying Lessons

Your first flying lesson begins with the instructor walking you around the airplane and explaining the parts, systems and controls. You wiggle the ailerons—at the back, outer edge of each wing—up and down and watch how, at the same time, the control yoke in the cockpit turns back and forth like a steering wheel. Behind the tail, you push the rudder back and forth. The instructor sends you to look inside the cockpit as he pushes on the rudder, and you notice the rudder pedals on the floor moving in and out as he moves the rudder left and right. At the same time, you discover that as the elevator moves up and down, the control yoke moves forward and backward.

With more strange terms than you can remember at first—pitot tube, static port, fuselage, empennage, horizontal and vertical stabilizers—you climb into the left seat, which is the pilot's seat of the aircraft, and your instructor confidently gets seated in the right seat. You are told you may rest your feet on the rudder pedals and your left hand on the control yoke in order to feel what the controls do as the instructor taxis, performs a pre-takeoff check of systems and engine, lines up for takeoff, rolls down the runway and lifts off the ground.

Your first flight is under the control of the instructor as you depart the airport area and climb to two or three thousand feet off the ground. Soon he turns over the controls to you, and you have some fun playing with the airplane. In the next lessons, you learn the fundamentals of flight: keep the airplane straight and level. You learn to turn and bank the airplane, to make it climb and glide, and finally to take off, fly the pattern around the airport and land smoothly. Repetition drills the procedures into your mental and physical memory, making each step of the checklist somewhat automatic.

POWERLESS

One day, on one of my training flights south of Olympia, Washington, flying over a rural area half covered with woods and half with fields, my instructor suddenly leaned over from the right seat and pulled the throttle all the way back, thus effectively reducing my power to nearly nothing. He pulled my power, first to see *how* I would react and second to teach me how I *should* react. In the air, if an engine quits, you pretty much are going to have one shot at any kind of landing, smooth or otherwise, and the student pilot practices emergency procedures so when the real thing happens, the response will be automatic.

What would you do? No matter how much experience and expertise you have, no matter if you are a beginner pilot or an astronaut, no power means your airplane's going down. What would your first reaction be? In that unexpected moment when my instructor pulled the power, my first reaction was to look outside for a place to land. That was natural. That was instinctive. That was a mistake—as he was about to explain.

That August day over northern Colorado, flying on fumes and a prayer, engine coughing and sputtering, propeller windmilling, I recalled the stern words of my flight instructor those years before when he first leaned over and pulled the power on my airplane just to see how I would react—three words that, up to now, meant something to me only during training flights. Otherwise, I'd never needed them before. But suddenly, in the moment of The Unexpected, these three words meant something to me in real life.

At the moment the engine coughed, those words zoomed to the forefront of my conscience thinking. If there had been any momentary shadow of hesitation, his instruction invaded my consciousness like a floodlight in a dark room. It all came back:

**"Bauer, when you lose power, and you're going down,
remember these three words and in this order:
Aviate, Navigate, Communicate."**

THREE WORDS

Aviate. Navigate. Communicate. In that order. Words drilled into memory by my flight instructor; words made permanent by many practice sessions in the air; words that now, flying on fumes and a prayer, became crucial for success and survival.

Aviate. Navigate. Communicate.

AVIATE

First things first: Aviate. Get control of the basics. The basics—keeping the airplane flying straight and level, establishing an appropriate airspeed for the inevitable descent, paying attention first of all to the airplane itself and maintaining control. Do not look out the window for a place to land ... not at first, anyway. Do not call on the radio for help or instructions or rescue or condolences ... not yet, anyway. Do not start pushing buttons or pulling controls or turning knobs or switching levers ... not yet anyway.

The basics are: Fly the plane! First and foremost, do not lose control of the airplane. The control yoke is in your hand, the rudder pedals under your feet ... use them to keep the plane under control. If you lose control, it won't matter where you might be able to land, and it won't matter that there's someone to talk to on the ground. If you lose control of the airplane, chances are it's all over for you. And that is not a good idea.

The first step you must take is: Control the basics. Aviate.

24

Navigate

Second things second: Navigate. When you've got control of the basics and the airplane is under your control, then Navigate. Get a picture in your mind of where you are, where you want to go, and how you're going to get there. Now you take a look outside, note your location, your direction and your altitude. Figure out where the best place would be for a landing. Is there a field, a beach, a road (hopefully without wires across it), a golf course, or best of all, an airstrip? How far away is it? Which direction should you land? Is the terrain sloping? Which way is the wind blowing across the ground? How should the approach be set up?

In the case of engine failure, you are like a glider, and you will have one shot at getting it right. There will be no second chance, no go-around, no mulligan—how you plan to get from where you are to where you want to go is critical. You will have one shot, and only one, at lining up and getting it right, at planning in a very short time for the best landing you can achieve under your circumstances.

The second step you must take is: Know where you are, where you want to go and how you're going to get there. Navigate.

Communicate

Third things third: Communicate. Use your radio to get in touch with someone on the ground. When someone sitting at a radar screen can see your blip, can see where you are and see where you want to go, they will be able to help you in several ways. They can give you wind direction and speed, they can give you advice for your circumstance, they can help keep you calm, they can notify other aircraft in the area as well as emergency personnel.

Even if you only make contact with someone at an airstrip somewhere beyond your landing range, you will be able to let them know where you are, that you are having difficulties and that you need help. In any case, having someone to talk to who's not emotionally involved helps you to think more calmly as you receive their advice and as they walk with you through your procedures.

The three words, in that order, add to each other. After getting control of the plane, you don't stop paying attention to Aviate while you plan your landing or contact someone via the radio. You don't stop flying your new route while you use your microphone and listen on your headset. First: Aviate—the basics. Then, after you have control of the airplane, add to that: Navigate. Finally, with the basics under control and with a navigational plan in place, add to that: Communicate.

Three words. Three words that flashed before the eyes of my ultra-alert mind. Three words I relied on over the next several minutes. Three words that, as you shall see, you can rely on for just about everything in life—particularly when The Unexpected happens.

THE UNEXPECTED

Oscar Wilde quipped, "To expect the unexpected shows a thoroughly modern intellect." By definition, you cannot know *what* will come at you, or when. By design, however, you *can* know how you will respond to The Unexpected. The irony is that you know The Unexpected will happen; that is not a surprise. Yet when it happens, it is a surprise. That The Unexpected will come is no surprise; *what, when, where* and *how* will be the surprise.

Can you be prepared for The Unexpected? Of course you can. The question is: will you be? "Aviate, Navigate, Communicate" came to my mind because of one thing: preparation. My instructor pulled the power during training not once, not twice, but many times, and always by surprise. We might have been practicing flying a circle around a point to learn to compensate for wind, and he would reach for the throttle and pull my power. We might have finished the day's lesson and be returning to the airport, and he would pull my power. Always in the back of my mind was stamped, "Aviate, Navigate, Communicate," the process by which I ensured my best chance of a successful emergency strategy. We trained deliberately so that I would react instinctively.

This is not the same as a "Plan B" because a backup plan is not for something unexpected. It is just another direction for which you plan ahead ... just in case Plan A is unsuccessful. In flying, a Plan B might include an alternate airport where you could land in case you encounter bad weather. You would know ahead of time where to land. In essence, Plan B is really just part of Plan A, an extension of the primary plan, or a fork in the road that you decide upon once you get there. If you get to a certain point down the road, you can take a look at circumstances and choose your pre-planned Plan B if you choose. There could even be a Plan C and a Plan D. These are simply contingency plans.

Nor is expecting The Unexpected the same as "we'll cross that bridge when we get to it." While that's the absence of a pre-planned Plan B, it still is an allowance for making up a Plan B on the fly, and you know ahead of time that the bridge is coming. For many of the ventures you embark on, making things up as you go might be the only way to make progress, especially if you are breaking new ground, making a first ascent ... or just don't like to ask for directions. Preparing for The Unexpected is simply knowing that eventually you will be surprised, blindsided or snuck up on.

BEST LAID PLANS

Two of my friends hiked the Wonderland Trail, a trek that encircles Mount Rainier over nearly a hundred miles of forests, streams and mountain meadows. Over the week it took to complete the trip, the pair carried everything they needed on their backs. Stopping at streams, they continued their faithful filtering of water for their water bottles so that no Giardia bacteria would be in their drinking water.

One of the ways you can spoil a mountain hiking trip is to drink unfiltered water. You can expect to entertain bugs like Giardia, bugs that will multiply in your intestinal tract and lead to what adventurists call "Montezuma's Revenge," "Beaver Fever" or simply "the trots." My friends filtered all their drinking water in order to avoid the discomfort, distraction and dismay that the Revenge would predictably produce. And yet ... even with such care, The Unexpected happened. About three-quarters of the way around the mountain, they both got slammed, and Montezuma got his revenge. This was not a Plan B event. Nor was this a "cross that bridge when we get to it" event, though you could argue that it might have been better at some particular bridge to have crossed it rather than stop at the be-germed waters underneath! This was The Unexpected.

THE UNEXPECTED

No matter how well laid are the plans of mice and men and mountain hikers, expect The Unexpected. While you will not know when it is coming or where, you can and should be prepared for it, and that's what this book is about.

When my engine coughed and sputtered over northern Colorado, that was, of course, not expected. That moment was not in my plans, not in a Plan B, not a contingency, and I certainly hadn't informed my passengers, "By the way, if we happen to run short on fuel and find ourselves going down, we'll just cross that bridge when we get to it." I had filled both fuel tanks before leaving the Mountain Home airport in Idaho. I had checked the en route weather and winds aloft. I knew the settings for fuel management. So it was a mysterious surprise that the fuel gauges were on empty. I should have had plenty of fuel for the flight. This was The Unexpected, come for a surprise visit like distant in-laws knocking at the door.

I did make a mistake. I should have informed Denver Control Center that I was changing my flight plan, and I should have descended for a landing and refueled at some airport in northern Colorado. By the clock, though, I still had fuel. When the direct route I'd been cleared for was altered due to changes in direction—being vectored around the skies as instructed by Denver Approach—more fuel was consumed. And I pushed on.

How about you? Has there been a time when you pushed on too long? Have you ignored warning signs? Has your vision for the goal been so clear, so intense, that you were like a horse wearing blinders? Malcolm Gladwell, in his book *Blink*, calls this, "mind blindness," a condition that makes normal people come to abnormal conclusions; people who interpret facts, for instance, in light of a desired outcome—because they *want* something to be a certain way, they filter facts narrowly and think logically to wrong conclusions. And so we fly on, we push ahead; we miss the signals around us or even those directly in front of us. Our intent is so focused we become myopic and tunnel-visioned. There is something to be said for focus, intent, drive and determination, but we simply must not lose our peripheral vision, our awareness of our surroundings and our circumstances while in hot pursuit of our objective. To ignore such is to invite trouble at best, disaster at worst.

BLAME

Finding a cause or someone to blame might be instructive for the future, but just at that moment when you're broadsided, when you run out of energy and you're going down, when you're faced with the need to react right now, searching for the cause won't help you. You need to know what action to take right at that moment, and you need to take that action.

The nature of blame is to find a cause and pin responsibility for something negative. Bad things happen, and when they do, it's typical not to want to look bad, not to shoulder responsibility. Nobody likes fingers pointed at them for bad things, so we act like a magician who misdirects the audience's attention by drawing their focus to something other than what he has up his sleeve. Likewise, we point elsewhere to take attention off of ourselves. And if we're not at fault, then we certainly don't want anyone to even *think* we might be at fault. Blaming is assigning responsibility for The Unexpected.

Can you imagine being a passenger aboard my flight, minding your own business, reading a book perhaps, and being jarred by the sound of sudden silence ... and hearing my first words: "Dang! They don't make fuel tanks like they used to." Or how about, "I told you guys not to bring so much luggage!" Would you care where I placed the blame? Do you think you would be concerned about the size or quality of the fuel tanks at that moment? Would you nod your head in agreement, turn to your fellow passengers and agree, "Yep, he told you not to bring all that stuff ... I told you to pack lighter! See? You've used up all our gas!" Probably you would not. I'm pretty sure your only concern would be that I keep you safe.

This is not the time for blame, not even if you blame yourself. You can do that later, if it becomes helpful for some reason to do so, but when The Unexpected hits, you'll be better served to deal with the immediate circumstances. When the unsinkable Titanic tore open its hull against an iceberg, it was simply and purely time to jump into the lifeboats.

Taking time to blame takes just that ... time. "There is a time for everything," says the author of Ecclesiastes, which by extension infers there is also a time *not* for everything. There is a time for war and a time for peace—but not at the same time. There is a time to plant and a time to uproot—but not at the same time. There is a time to be silent and a time to speak—but again, not at the same time. When The Unexpected hits, it's time for immediate and decisive action, it's time to draw on your training and experience, it's time for

Aviate, Navigate, Communicate. There's a time for action and a time for reflection—but not at the same time.

Stop blaming, focus on the facts, act now.

FIRST SOLO

On this wet morning as I accelerate down Runway Three-Zero at La Grande/Union County Airport for my first solo flight, with just seven hours of instruction logged in my logbook, I am fully alive. There is not a nerve or muscle or bone in my body that is not awake to the adventure. If you are watching from the flight office, everything appears rather ho-hum. Airplanes take off all the time. Kind of boring, actually. But inside that little Cessna 152, it was me and the wild blue yonder. I might as well be Hillary and Norgay taking those last steps up Everest, becoming the first in history to stand on the highest patch of snow on the highest mountain in the world. I might as well be Neil Armstrong standing on the lowest rung of the ladder alongside the lunar lander, about to take that giant leap for mankind. This is personal, my own quest to go where no man has gone before.

Actually, many have gone there before. But I never have. And because it is my first venture alone in the cockpit of the airplane, it feels no differently for me than if I actually was the first one ever to lift off the ground in a heavier-than-air powered flying machine. My machine and I accelerate down the runway. The nose lifts as I pull back slowly on the control yoke. I lose sight of the runway under the nose cowl, and I feel the rumble of the main wheels as they begrudge the effort of the wings lifting them from the asphalt. Suddenly, it is smooth. The power of lift overcomes the power of gravity, and I— I am flying solo!

THE UNEXPECTED

As during practice flights, I climb to five hundred feet above the ground, bank left, continue climbing, check to my right and left for other airplanes before making the next left at about a thousand feet above the ground. No time in my life matches the combined exhilaration, apprehension and alertness as at this moment. The Unexpected could show up—unexpectedly. The engine could quit. Another airplane could cut me off. My radio chatter might be incorrect, thereby both embarrassing myself and confusing other pilots who, in their confusion (or laughter) might miss seeing me and collide. Anything could happen.

I continue the downwind leg at a thousand feet off the ground, paralleling the runway in the opposite direction of takeoff and running through the mental checklist of events that must happen in the next couple of minutes. Things usually happen very slowly at altitude, cruising far above the ground, traveling from one point to the next, as long as there are no emergencies. But in the landing pattern, next to the airport, with only seven hours under your belt, things happen fast and without concern for whether you are ready or not. I am embarrassed by my white knuckles, but no one else can see them, nor will anyone ever know.

I pass the end of Runway Three-Zero, opposite the starting point of the first solo trip I have ever taken anywhere on the planet, and I start my descent. "Please God … don't let me forget anything!" Reduce power, lower flaps ten degrees, pull carburetor ice control knob, maintain heading, let airspeed reduce. Looking back over my left shoulder, I wait for the runway numbers at the runway threshold to be about forty-five degrees behind me, and then bank left from the downwind leg to the crosswind leg.

The section of the pattern where you fly with the wind coming at you from the side, before the last turn to final approach, is called the crosswind leg. Flaps further extended. Power reduced. Airspeed reduced. Check for traffic to my right—no one else is coming in for a landing. "Thank you, God!" A final bank to the left for the last leg— the final approach. Extend flaps fully, adjust power, maintain airspeed, line up with the runway center line, announce on radio, "Cessna 92582 ... short final ... Runway Three-Zero." Expect The Unexpected. Consciously reduce tension in hands, lighten grip on control yoke. Cross runway threshold, begin to pull back on control yoke to flare airplane just above runway. Rudder control. Elevator control. Wings level.

The stall warning horn begins its eerie wail and moments later, in a synchronous sense of sound and settling, the tires screech and ... well, they bounce. They bounce hard, sending the airplane back up into the air and somewhat sideways, directly over the white centerline, but not precisely parallel to it. It's The Unexpected. It's called "ballooning." And I balloon big time. I balloon embarrassingly big time. I sense I'm out of control. Then gravity takes over with a vengeance and draws me without hesitation back to the asphalt runway, still not lined up well and still with too much speed. I balloon a second time, bouncing into the air above the runway. The airspeed bleeds off inevitably, I drop the remaining two feet to the runway like a dead duck, except I am rolling down the runway ... at least parallel with, and not too far from, the white line. Somewhere in a back room of my brain, I wonder if anyone can see me from the flight office. I have hoped for a certain amount of dignity, but dignity has eluded me for the moment.

But I am back on the ground; I have completed my first solo takeoff and landing—more or less gracefully. I am still breathing, and the airplane is still running, rolling down the runway in fact, waiting for me to do something before we run out of runway. Flaps up, full power, pick up speed down the runway, and when I reach the right airspeed, I pull the nose up and I am in the air, solo, to fly the pattern again.

I repeat the process, and the third landing is actually pretty good. I taxi the plane to the tie-down area, and as I turn everything off I notice the flight office door open as my flight instructor comes out to meet and congratulate me. He takes a Polaroid picture of me standing by the white airplane with its yellow stripes and large N-number painted on its side. I say I hope he didn't see the landings. He did.

Logbook entry—

Date: October 4.

Place: La Grande to La Grande.

Flight time: one hour.

Dual time: forty minutes.

Solo time: twenty minutes.

Twenty glorious, wonderful, exhilarating minutes.

It was different several years later over northern Colorado in Cessna November-One-Zero-Six-Five-Victor. Knuckles were no longer white—even bouncing around in the clouds was taken in stride. I had many hours of solo flight logged in my logbook. I was a commercially-licensed, instrument rated pilot (though newly instrument rated). There had been lots more instruction in a wide variety of circumstances since that day I flew my first solo flight, and some of those hours had been spent in practicing emergency procedures. Always in the back of a pilot's mind, on call, is the readiness to respond to The Unexpected. But again, unexpected events are—The Unexpected!

When you fly a single-engine airplane and your single engine quits, the sound is, as they say, deafening. It is startling. The Unexpected blasts a clarion call to every sense of your being, and its appeal to instant and appropriate action is compelling. Readiness becomes alert and active. There is little time to think, to reason, to run down checklists.

At the moment my engine quit, I did not have time to reflect on what caused it. I did not have time to review what put me in the situation. I did not have time to blame. I only had time to react, and to react quickly.

———————————

"...AVIATE, NAVIGATE, COMMUNICATE.

AND IN THAT ORDER!"

Logbook

FUMES *and a* PRAYER

CHAPTER THREE

AVIATE

a-vi-ate *verb* \'ā-vē-,āt\

operate an aircraft; fly

FUMES *and a* PRAYER

How do you feel, five thousand feet above the ground in a small airplane with a single engine, and that single engine quits? The man to my right was certainly excited. He turned around to his napping wife, woke her up and pointed out the fuel gauges, which were still on empty. I've never figured out why he didn't let his wife sleep peacefully through the event, but apparently he wanted company as he was freaking out.

A small group of seventh-grade girls asked me once, when I told them I'd run out of fuel flying a six-passenger airplane to Denver. "What did you do?" they asked.

I responded, "What would *you* do?"

The instant reply: "Scream!!!"

"Really?" I said. "You'd really want your pilot to scream?"

I was outwardly calm, controlled—no matter what the circumstances, you do not want your pilot to panic. Still, I had no idea how much fuel was in the other tank. The left tank was dry, and I quickly leaned down and flipped the fuel selector valve to the right tank.

The fuel-injected engine on this airplane, I'd been told, was not known to be an easy one to restart in the air, and a successful re-start depended on having enough fuel to get it started in the first place. I needed two things at that moment: enough fuel in the right tank to feed the engine, and a cooperative engine. If the engine started, we could continue on for a short bit at least. If not, the rest of our trip was going to be very short.

Aviate. Fly the plane. Forget for the moment about looking for a place to land, forget about going through checklists to figure out what went wrong, forget about calling on the radio. Fly the plane. First and foremost, get control of the plane. Don't be like a student I once had who, when I simulated losing an engine by pulling the throttle back to idle, immediately began to flip switches, pull levers and turn knobs, completely without thought and totally in panic. When you do that it's easy to forget about the most important thing, the basic thing: Fly the plane!

BASICS

Driving home from Seattle one stormy night, my oldest daughter was in the driver's seat of my Chevy Astro van. She was the holder of a driver's permit. I wanted her to get as much driving time as possible because I figured the more experience she had, the more likely she would drive safely. In the far left lane, southbound on Interstate 5, traffic was moderately heavy—but the biggest challenge was the rain. As we approached a downpour at sixty miles an hour, we were about to pass through the road spray from a semi on our right when, at the same time, we hit accumulated water on the night-black roadway. She began to panic as everything happened at once.

I was myself a touch nervous, but I told her, "Just keep us between the white lines." Focused on the most basic aspect of automotive navigation, keeping the van between the white lines, she successfully passed the truck, maintained control and got us out of danger.

That is focusing on the basics, and it is the first thing you must do when The Unexpected hits you. It is extremely important that you focus on the basics first and avoid the temptation to look at navigational issues or to start asking people what to do. You'll do that, of course, but not as your first step.

A Chicago airport tower records a chilling distress call from a panicked pilot. The pilot radios the tower. His voice is desperate and panicked.

"Help! Help," he shouts. His radio clicks off.

The tower controller responds, asking the nature of the pilot's problem.

"Help! Help! I'm in a spin! Help me!" he cries again.

A spin means the aircraft is corkscrewing downward. It is deadly if the pilot does not gain control of his airplane before it hits the ground.

The tower answers again, suggesting that the pilot try to stay calm. The pilot is anything but calm.

Totally stressed and disoriented, he calls again, "Help me!"

The controller knows the best solution, "Let go of the controls, sir. Let go of the controls."

That might seem crazy to most people, but many modern, recreational light planes are built with a safety feature—if the airplane goes into a spin, and if the pilot lets go of the controls, the airplane will automatically recover from the spin. If there's enough altitude for the airplane to do that, then letting go of the controls might save the pilot's life.

The pilot on the radio cries out one more time, "Help, He....." His radio goes eerily silent.

Several calls from the tower controller go unanswered and it becomes obvious that the pilot did not survive.

Aviate. Fly the plane.

Whether driving a car or flying an airplane, whether climbing a mountain or scuba diving, whether starting a business or getting married—if you start with the basics, you have the best chance of survival. The basics of a house are its foundation and frame. Get that right and you finish out a sturdy home that's able to withstand a lot of wind and rain. Get it wrong and it won't matter how pretty the cabinets and doors are—its longevity may be reduced by years.

The basics of a car are its chassis, engine and drive train. Built well, you have a solid car. The two basic elements of a relationship and a marriage are the level and quality of its friendship and the ability to repair those inevitable clashes. Destroy the qualities of friendship, fail at repairing clashes, and you lose the relationship.

A wise, sensible person "built his house on a rock ... The rain fell, the rivers rose, the winds pounded on the house. But it did not collapse, because its foundation was on the rock."—Jesus, Sermon on the Mount.

Basics matter.

AVIATE

"AVIATE" IN BUSINESS

Aviate—to get control of the basics—is fundamental and foundational. In business, it's not how the daily business operates, it's not the office décor, it's not the dress code. Business elements like these have their place, of course, but they should not be the foundation of your business. The basics of a business are its product or service, and its cash flow. Keep control of these first of all; keep them in the air, flying straight and level. They are your business's foundation.

If you're not the owner or manager of the business, and you punch a time clock every day like I did at Boeing, your job still entails these foundation blocks. When I installed parts on a Boeing 707 as part of the aerial tanker production line, I had, in essence, my own little "business." One of my products was the window assembly and installation in the lower part of the tail of the airplane where a future boom operator would lay prone, extending the winged boom with a fuel nozzle at the end, watching the aircraft just below and behind the tanker plane and guiding the nozzle to the fuel intake port on the other plane—all at altitude and at cruising airspeed. My window was a critical installation. Without that window, the boom operator would be blind, like driving down the highway without a windshield.

I received the window for my "business" from the window shop, and I had to make sure it was built to specifications so it would fit the frame where I would install it. My product, the window, had to be installed in a certain amount of time. I was paid by the hour, so there was a cash flow issue for Boeing—taking too long cost them more money. I "sold" my product first to the inspector, then to the next crew down the production line. If I did a poor job with my product, the inspector wouldn't buy it, and if I somehow got an improper installation past the inspector (which never happened, of course, because I always did a good job ... except for one time, as you'll see), then the next crew would have to deal with a bad product. They would likely complain, first of all, and then return it. More cash flow issues would result as I took time to repair it.

The glass in the window was about two feet wide, a foot high and something like an inch thick. The frame around it was solid, heavy aluminum. Engineering drawings, or blueprints, indicated exactly where to install the rivets to fasten the window frame to the aircraft structure. I measured and marked the location of the holes, drilled through the exact spots and positioned the window in place with temporary, removable fasteners. I placed an aluminum rivet into a hole and with my rivet gun and bucking bar, secured the rivet in place.

A bucking bar is a hand-held, solid block of steel in various sizes and shapes to get behind the tail of the rivet, sometimes in tight spots, so when the rivet gun pounds on the head side of the rivet, the steel bucking bar flattens the tail of the aluminum rivet. There were a good number of rivets holding that window assembly to the airplane.

One day, as I worked across the top of the window frame, with holes drilled and ready for rivets, I held the rivet gun in my right hand, pushed a rivet through a hole over the center of the window, grabbed a bucking bar that weighed about a pound with my left hand, lifted it up to get behind the frame and structure ... but didn't quite make it all the way to the top of the window before I bumped something with my left elbow, lost my grip on the bucking bar which, unfortunately, at that moment was directly over the center of the window itself.

AVIATE

This is one of those moments that can be described in detail in several sentences, that can be seen in detail and replayed in slow motion, but in real time, in a nanosecond, it occurred in the blink of an eye. My eyes really did blink. Several times. I dropped that bucking bar directly in the middle of the glass window and the window responded instantaneously by cracking—not the kind of crack you get on your windshield when you're dinged by a rock, but the kind you get when you drop a hard boiled egg from the ceiling to the floor. There were hundreds of cracks! Maybe thousands. Somehow, not one piece of glass fell out of the frame to the concrete floor fifteen feet below, but if the window had fallen, I doubt there could have been any more pieces on the floor than were already in the broken window. I don't know what held it together.

At that moment I had no idea what the cash value of the window was. As I recall, I was told later that the cost was something like fifteen thousand dollars. I couldn't calculate how many paychecks that would be, but I knew it was a lot of hamburgers! My heart sank. This obviously affected both product and cash flow for Boeing, and perhaps it would affect my cash flow as well.

It was just before lunch time. I crawled out of the boom operator compartment with a great deal of reluctance and regret, and I told my crew chief and my supervisor what happened. To their credit, neither man yelled at me. We all walked to the airplane, crawled down into the compartment and gazed at the damage. The window was way beyond repair—it would have to be replaced. I think that's when I asked them how much the window cost.

They knew how badly I felt, and they probably saw a combination of guilt, dismay and fear on my face. They took the attitude that accidents happen. They told me to go have lunch, come back afterward and remove the window. They ordered a new assembly and simply told me that if anything like this happened again I would be reprimanded, and a third offense would result in dismissal.

As a "business," my product was the window assembly. I received it, installed it, and sold it to the next crew on the assembly line. My cash flow, as an hourly employee, was my paycheck—but in a way, time was cash. If you look at it that way, my cost was the time I spent receiving, installing and selling my product. Most of the time things went very well, and the window, along with other parts and assemblies I installed, was profitable—I sold a great product to a satisfied customer in a short amount of time.

Whether you're the owner, or the employee, keep control of your product or service, and your cash flow. The basics.

Processes

In business, a company has its "business operations" or, more specifically, its "operational processes" by which it keeps alive the "core business," its main activity. There are other processes as well, such as managerial processes, sales processes and accounting processes, but for the moment let's look just at the production of the company's product or service.

In 1776, Adam Smith, often described as the father of modern economics and capitalism, took a look at the processes involved in the production of a simple pin by dividing the process into approximately eighteen sub-tasks: draw out the wire, straighten the wire, cut the wire, point the wire, grind the top of the wire for receiving the pin head, fasten the pin head, whiten the pin, and so on.

Whether your business is making pins, fixing cars, building websites, running backhoes, selling homes or leading adventure expeditions, you have processes by which you operate your business. Spelling these processes out is like having an instruction manual for your business.

The two foundations of your business—product or service, and cash flow—can be split into four areas of operations. An MBA will likely cringe at my simplicity, but for a small business owner, simplicity is a friend. Here, I'll refer to both a product and a service simply as the product. The four operations are:

1. Purchasing (getting what you need to make your product or to provide your service),

2. Manufacturing (making your product),

3. Advertising and Marketing (letting people know that the product is available and that it's something people want), and

4. Sales (transferring items of value—I give you the product or service, you give me the money).

Again, there are other aspects to your business—finances and record-keeping, for example—but if something unexpected happens to your business, you'll need to quickly and purposefully direct your attention to what it is that keeps you flying in the first place.

In a small business or a home-based business, defining these production processes is an often overlooked practice. Often, the entrepreneur knows how to repair a car or how to build a website or how to operate a backhoe. The problem most business startups face, as Michael Gerber puts it in his best-selling book, *The E-Myth*, is that a technician believes that he or she can turn their skill or knowledge into a business simply because they know how to do the activity. The backhoe operator with ten years of experience has worked for a contractor all those years and one day decides he would rather not punch a time clock nor receive an hourly wage from someone else— why not do it independently, be your own boss, go into business for yourself! "After all," says the backhoe operator, "I'm really good at what I do, and fast too. I can do this business myself."

But that's a myth, according to Gerber. To run a backhoe does require knowledge and experience running a backhoe. But to do it as a business requires knowledge and experience in business, and one must decide whether they want to run backhoes or to run a business that runs backhoes.

Do you see the difference? You either run a backhoe or you run a business. You either work on cars or you work on a business. You either build websites or you build a business. Of course, if you are the only person in your company, you are the one doing the technical work. The difference is both in viewpoint and in purpose. As I learned from Gerber, you work either *in* your business or you work *on* your business. You are an employee in your own company, or you are a business owner who happens to work for your business. If you don't distinguish between the two, and you see yourself primarily as the doer of the work rather than the owner of the business, you are likely to fail—not because you can't do the work, but because you are not running the business as a business. Otherwise you are focused on things other than the basic processes, and that's something you need to change.

CORE ACTIVITY

Big companies as well as small entrepreneurships all have a "core activity," and while big companies have MBAs to help define what that activity is, a small business owner should define the core activity for himself. It may take some thought, some analysis, to truly define what it is you do, but if you write it out you will have the most fundamental aspect of your business, that upon which you must focus especially when you are blindsided by an unexpected trial.

If your foundation is the combination of your product and cash flow, then what is it you are building upon that foundation? Every business is built on product and cash flow—or it should be—if it isn't, then it's time for some immediate and extensive excavation to put in a solid foundation. The difference between businesses is what's built on top of that foundation. What you build on top of the foundation is your core, the framework that holds every room and every wall and every door and every window of your business in place.

When I received my real estate agent license, I noticed many hungry agents who took any type of client and any type of sale in any area of real estate. They might have had a client who wanted to sell their home, another client who wanted to sell their business, another client who wanted to buy a commercial building and yet another client who wanted to buy bank-owned investment properties. Add townhouses, condominiums, vacant land, new construction communities, fixer-uppers … agents spread themselves so thin trying to keep track of such a variety of transactions that some clients cannot possibly receive adequate or competent service. That's because the agent does not have a "core" business. Was it legal for a licensed agent to offer service in all those areas? Yes, at least in my state. Was it wise? I don't think so.

After I started my video production company, I visited the local technical college where there was a video production department. I am, for better or for worse, a hands-on sort of entrepreneur. I jump into something with keen interest and bright vision.

One of my daughters once told me, as I considered trying something new, "Dad, we've never done that before!"

I said, "So? Since when has that ever stopped us?"

But then I also jump into some intensive self-learning. I read books, I search online, I ask a lot of questions of knowledgeable people. That's why I visited the tech college instructors. Just because you haven't done something before, doesn't mean you shouldn't try it.

Along with a lot of technical advice about equipment and technique, I was offered this broad bit of advice, "Take any job you can get as long as it's moral and legal." My problem, in the beginning of my video career, was that I took that advice. I shot weddings, I shot sports, I shot promotions, I shot how-to videos ... as long as it wasn't immoral or illegal, I shot it. I hope you understand that when I say I shot Kenny G (which I did), or I shot the governor of the State of Washington, or I shot the host of The 700 Club, or I shot the bride and groom ... everybody lived! I got them all on tape ... no weapons involved. (I do get surprised looks when I use the term "shot" in reference to whomever it was I shot.)

The problem is that I became moderately good at a variety of video production jobs, but I was expert at only one. I got really good at taping figure skaters at ice skating competitions all over the country. We enjoyed a great reputation. When we set up our order table in preparation for a competition, I loved to hear comments like, "Oh! Bauer Video! Good ... glad you're the ones doing this competition!" Indeed, as time went on, I had about ninety-five percent of market-share in the northwestern states of Washington, Oregon and Idaho. Everything else I did was fluff. I did my best, but shooting weddings was not my core business, and it would have served me better to stick just to the core.

What is the core of your business? With a clear definition of what is at the core of your business, you will not be tempted to immediately look for new directions when things get tight. Examining new directions might be a necessary second step, but not the first thing to do. Nor will you be calling on friends for advice while you spin out of control. You will need to look first at keeping yourself in the air—you will look first at the basics of your business, its core activity, and you will turn your focus on that. Remember, "Aviate, Navigate, Communicate, and in that order!"

In real estate, perhaps you should consider just residential sales and get really, really good at it. Or land sales. Or investment properties. I believe you will make much more money by specializing and becoming the best in that one core area, than you will by trying to take on anything as long as it's moral and legal. Just because you *can* do something, doesn't mean you should.

I asked my friend David, who owns Bill's Boathouse on American Lake in Lakewood, Washington—where I sit at this moment glancing from my laptop to more than twenty-five feet of wall-to-wall, floor to ceiling windows, just twenty feet from the lake's edge—what is the core business of Bill's Boathouse. He knew immediately. It's not the banquet room, where I sit, it's not the boat slip rental on his dock, it's not book sales, it's not boat sales. His core business is serving people who fish. Dave could be focusing on any of the other activities of a boathouse that sits on a beautiful lake, but he doesn't. He focuses on the core business of serving people who like to fish.

The point is that you too need to be able to define your core business. If you don't, you will dilute your efforts, thinly spreading your time and money and other resources in efforts that you will do only moderately well. I'm convinced that when you lay a rock-solid foundation of product and cash flow, and build a solid frame, which is your core business, and keep your focus on that, then you provide yourself a high likelihood of success in your endeavor. You will have control of the basics, and that's where it all starts, and that's what will keep you flying when you are hit by The Unexpected.

If you have a small business, what is its core activity? Write it out in one sentence on the Logbook page at the end of this chapter. Then the hard question: can you define your operations in terms of purchasing, manufacturing, marketing/advertising and sales? For each area, write out, step-by-step, what those operational activities are. These are your basics. Aviate means that when things are going well, you are doing these activities. Aviate also means that when The Unexpected happens, you fall back to getting control of the basics. Fly the plane! Fly your business!

If your business is messed up, and if there's any hope of keeping it flying, then before you do anything else … define your core business, redirect your resources to that core, make your product the best it can be and don't spend more money than you make so you maintain a positive cash flow. First and foremost, keep your business in the air. Get control of the basics. Fly the plane!

THE ONE THING

In the movie *City Slickers*, Curly (Jack Palance) is giving Mitch (Billy Crystal) advice on life. Curly asks Mitch if he knows what the secret of life is, and he holds up one finger. "One thing," Curly tells Mitch. There's just one thing, and it's the only thing that matters. Mitch is curious and asks what the "one thing is," and Curly answers by telling Mitch that's what he's got to figure out.

That *is* what you have to find out because that one thing is what you must do when The Unexpected hits you hard. That one thing is your best hope of survival. That one thing is what will keep you in the air, will set the stage for your next steps, and will keep everything else intact.

If you don't know what the basics are for you, what the core activity is, when The Unexpected happens you have little hope in anything ... other than luck. You might as well support your home state by buying lottery tickets—the chance of success is about the same.

If you have never defined what the basics are for you, I urge you to stop right now and work this out on paper.

1.   What is the core thing for you? If you own a business, what do you do? If you are in a relationship, what is the one thing that keeps it healthy? If you are on an adventure, what is the main thing that will keep you alive when things go wrong so you can tell about it when you are back home at the dinner table?

2.   What are the basic operational systems that must be working at all times, without which you will nosedive if you are hit by The Unexpected? Even relationships have systems. Think about the way you communicate. That's a system. What about making plans for a trip or a dinner out? That's another system. Who does what chores, when do they need to be done and how often? Another system. Raising, teaching and disciplining children ... more systems. Write these out.

3. What experiences have you already had that inform your decisions above? Write out at least one anecdote for each, more if you can. Put all this into a notebook or journal so it can be reviewed, revised and refined.

When you are hit by The Unexpected, having too much information keeps you from focusing on these basics. That's exactly why you need to know what the basics are and why you stay away from Navigation and Communication as first steps. If you can't say what the core things are for your business, for a relationship or for an adventure, then it's easy to succumb to information overload since you are likely to energetically start running to and fro in an effort to find anything you can hang onto, grasping for a handhold anywhere you can find one.

This is because, as Malcolm Gladwell explains in detail in his book, *Blink*, we tend to think best in "thin slices," micro-second insights that provide us with our first impressions. It usually does not take knowing all the details in order to make a good decision. Of all the information available to you, most of the time all you need is a thin slice of that information to judge correctly what you need to do. Too much information is like an overpowered, off-road vehicle in mud … you spin your wheels because there's too much energy to escape the mire.

Aviate, in a crisis, takes advantage of that thin bit of essential information or foundational skill that comes from your planning, experience and practice, and that is at the core of what you do. The core skills in flying an airplane are straight and level flight, turns, climbs and glides. The core elements in a pancake business (I'm guessing) might be the mix of ingredients and the temperature of the frying pan. The core elements of a relationship are friendship and repairs. What is at the core of your endeavor, your venture, or your adventure?

The core items for survival in the mountains, as taught by The Mountaineers Club, the third largest outdoor recreation club of its kind in the United States, are the "Ten Essentials." This is the list I received when I took a mountaineering course from the club as a junior in high school:

1. Map
2. Compass
3. Sunglasses and sunscreen
4. Extra clothing
5. Headlamp/flashlight
6. First-aid supplies
7. Fire starter
8. Matches
9. Knife
10. Extra food

The purpose for the ten items collectively is to enable you to handle an accident or emergency, and to stay more than a day in safety. In other words, this well-known list, developed in the 1930s, is what you need if The Unexpected happens in the mountains. It's likely you'll need most or all of them for a normal outing in the mountains. It's definite you'll need them in an emergency. The list of essential items might be adapted or updated over time, but the point is that you have the basic tools you need for survival, especially when the availability of drive-through fast food is nowhere in sight!

Will you take more stuff with you into the mountains? You probably will. No mention is made in the basic list of the myriad selections of freeze-dried foods, for instance, nor the styles of lightweight gas stoves you might choose from. There's nothing about what materials your climbing boots might be made of, no mention of synthetic rope materials, not a word about Gore-Tex or breathability factors in parkas. The information cataloged about all that stuff is interesting reading before a trip into the hills, and it would be wise to be well informed before making purchases, but if an unexpected storm attacks and you are pinned down for a few extra days and nights, you'd better have the extra clothes and food at hand. It's basics time.

When my engine quit, I automatically knew what to do first. I knew the core elements of flying, the essentials, the basics. I paid attention to the wings, kept them level and, although we would expect to lose some altitude, I made sure we maintained our heading, flying straight and keeping the airplane under control. Basics.

Like a seasoned boxer who spars and jabs and feints and defends, all without thinking, I automatically reached down with my right hand to the floor of the airplane for the red fuel selector valve handle. It pointed at a forty-five degree angle to the left, toward the now be-fumed left fuel tank. I turned it clockwise to point toward the right fuel tank; the valve handle stopped in its detent, forty-five degrees to the right.

AVIATE

If there was anything more than fumes and a prayer in the right tank, I needed it right now. I needed fuel in the lines, at the valve and in the fuel pump, which forced it through the injectors and into the engine cylinders—to be ignited by the electrical spark from each of two spark plugs in every cylinder, and in the explosion within those cylinder walls, like a patient on a paramedic's gurney who receives an electrical shock from the paramedic's paddles to restart his heart, I needed the engine to resuscitate.

In the olden days, before electric starters, you started a car by turning a crank handle in front of the car. That turned the crankshaft, pumped fuel into the carburetor which sprayed a fuel/air mixture into the cylinders, and also turned the generator (in the days before alternators) which provided spark to the spark plugs—each action combining to fire up the engine. Cranking the engine by hand got it all started.

My airplane's propeller should have the same effect. Like a pinwheel held out the car window, the air moving past the curved blades of the propeller made it spin, or "windmill," and I hoped that would be enough to crank the engine back to life.

FUMES *and a* PRAYER

Logbook

CHAPTER FOUR

NAVIGATE

nav-i-gate *verb* \'na-və-,gāt\

plan and follow a course

FUMES *and a* PRAYER

In similar situations, as I found out later, other pilots had difficulty getting this type of engine restarted in the air. At the time, I didn't know that. Apparently this engine didn't know that either. The windmilling propeller continued to crank the engine—turning the crankshaft over and over, pumping the pistons, powering the fuel pump, and sucking any fuel that remained in the right tank. Under the cowling, all three hundred energized horses escaped the starting gate of the Preakness, and like a faithful horse that jumps to action at the heel kick of its rider, my engine jumped to life.

A sense of instant gratification shot through every cell of my body, every nook and cranny of mind and soul and spirit. I was as alive as those horses in my engine.

I mentally breathed a huge sigh of relief when the engine restarted. I'm sure my passengers felt the same, though the story could be enhanced if at this point they had heartily cheered and if they had gratefully slapped my back and if they had given lavished compliments—"Atta boy, captain! Way to save our lives!"

But they pretty much just sat there. I'm not sure why, but that's what they did. Never mind—my engine was running, I was under power, and we were not going down. Not yet.

That was the good news. The bad news was…

...we were not yet on the ground. Just because the engine restarted did not mean we were clear of the emergency. The facts still stared at me from those two fuel gauges—somehow the fuel had been used much too quickly, and the needle on the right fuel gauge was showing that the right tank was as empty as the left. How much fuel was left in that right tank? We were flying with power at the moment, but how many moments were left before the right tank was down to just fumes and my engine stopped again? There was only one way to find out.

I knew now that I shouldn't try to get from where I was to where I wanted to go. I needed a new place to land. With the airplane under control, I began the second of the three words: Navigate.

URGENCY

If you've faced an emergency where time is of the essence then you've known that gripping urgency of doing something in a hurry. Diversions are not welcome. When you're flying on fumes and a prayer, you want to point your nose to the nearest fuel stop and fly a beeline to your landing spot. If you drive around town with the gas gauge below the empty mark, maybe you pray the foxhole prayer, "God, if you get me out of this..." or "If you get me to a gas station...." Even if you usually look for the cheapest gas in town, you head for the closest gas station to get a few dollars of gas, no matter what the price.

Run out of gas on the road ... you pull over. Run out of gas in the air ... you're going down. If you're several thousand feet off the ground and your fuel gauges are reading empty, the impetus to get to an airport for fuel becomes urgent.

My plan to proceed to Arapahoe County Airport was abandoned. I was still a half hour away ... plus it would take several more minutes to set up an approach, fly the pattern and land at Arapahoe.

Denver Approach Control started instructing me to fly in various directions, a normal procedure when approaching a busy airport to avoid any close calls between us private planes and the big-brother jets in the sky. It's called "vectoring." But for me it was like praying my way to a gas station and hitting red lights all along the way. In Cessna N1065V, the radio chatter was something like:

Denver Approach: *"Turn left to heading zero-niner-zero."*
Me: *"Zero-niner-zero. Roger."*
A couple minutes later:
Denver Approach: *"Turn right to heading one-seven-zero. Descend and maintain seven thousand feet."*
Me: *"One-seven-zero. Descend to seven thousand feet. Roger."*
After several more minutes:
Denver Approach: *"Turn left to heading one-three-five."*
Me: *"One-three-five. Roger."*
A minute later:
Denver Approach: *"Turn right to heading one-five-zero."*
Me: *"One-five-zero. Roger."*

Gas gauge on empty … drive a block, hit a red light. Wait. Drive two blocks, hit a red light. Wait. Drive a block. Hit a red light. Wait. It was like that.

At the other end of the radio chatter, an FAA air traffic controller at Denver Approach Control sat, I assumed, in a government-issued chair, wearing a ball cap and a two-way headset and staring at a green radar screen. The rotating line blipped all air traffic in the area he was watching. I was one of those blips. The air traffic controller likely had a coffee cup at his console. I'm sure the focus was sharp on his end, as it should be. But his feet were on the ground. My feet were on a pair of rudder pedals, with a great deal of vertical space between me and the ground. And as I sped through the air at something like 170 miles an hour, not knowing how close the right tank was to holding nothing but fumes, my navigational needs at that point required a different approach. I could not continue to be vectored around the skies somewhere north of Denver.

There are three components to Navigation: where you are, where you want to end up, and the route that connects the dots from where you are to where you want to go. That may seem obvious, but accurately defining the three components may not be so easy when it comes to business or relationships or adventures or becoming a better speaker—whatever your endeavor.

Now, if all you want to do is take a Sunday drive and all you know is that the starting point of the venture is your driveway, then the destination won't be defined as a point on the map, but there is still a destination of sorts. Your objective might be enjoyment, relaxation, time with family, or collecting photographs of fall colors, and that objective defines your "destination." If you arrive back home in the evening, and you are relaxed, or you collected some great photos, then you reached your objective, your destination. Your route in this case would be determined on the fly.

For most ventures, however, you have a starting point, an ending point, and a route between the two. That is the essence of Navigate. Of course there's a lot more of both art and science to navigation, but when you take the concept down to its basic essence, that's it.

THE A-B-Cs OF NAVIGATE

You start somewhere—that's where you are. It's either the starting point of the journey, or it's the place where you are at this moment.

You go somewhere—that's where you want to be. It's the ending point of the journey

And you decide upon a course that will get you from where you are to where you want to be. It's the step-by-step list of dots that get you there.

That's the ABCs of Navigate:

A = where you Are
B = where you want to Be
C = the Course you will take from A to B.

This assumes, naturally, that you know where you are. Not knowing where you are means you are lost, or as I like to say, "I'm not lost ... I just don't know where I am." Ego aside, I'm lost.

Without knowing "A" (where you Are), knowing "B" (where you want to Be) is irrelevant because you can't know "C" (the Course to take between A and B). It's a three-part equation, but in this case, knowing B and C won't give you A.

Lost? Then let's start with A: "Where you Are."

A: The "Where You Are" Component"

"Well, I'm right here," you might say, as if knowing where your feet are planted at the moment is all you need to know when you start a journey. Knowing your location on a GPS is one aspect of your starting point, but it is far from complete and you're going to need to know a whole lot more than that.

At point A you do need to take stock of location. You also need to take stock of all the assets and resources you have available to you at that time, as well as what your conditions are and what the positives and negatives are. It's all part of your starting point.

If you meet me at the local airport for a flight across the state and into Idaho, say, to go camping and fishing in the mountains for a weekend, certain elements of planning had better be determined before we even get in the airplane and head out the taxiway.

Every airplane has a limit on the weight it can safely carry aloft. Besides the aircraft's empty weight, there are fuel tanks carrying avgas, which is aviation fuel, at six pounds per gallon. The Cessna I flew that day over northern Colorado holds 65 gallons. That's 390 pounds of fuel in the tanks. Then there are passengers. If the actual weight of passengers is not known (I've never actually felt confident in asking!), then the standard figure in aviation circles is 180 pounds per person aboard. If all seats were filled in the 6-seat Cessna 206, then that's 1,080 pounds. Then there is baggage. For our trip to Idaho, that includes our personal belongings, our camping and fishing gear, the actual fish if we're successful, and ice to carry the fish back in.

The weight of the aircraft's load is critical to know before you lift off the ground because, if it's over the limit, the aircraft may lift off the ground just from the effect of wind flowing over the wings and pushing the aircraft off the runway, what pilots call "ground effect"—but when the airplane is several feet off the ground and loses the ground effect, the aircraft will likely stall and fall to the ground. That's a situation we tend to want to avoid. So a pilot needs to know the weight of the load he's asking the airplane to carry.

Equally important is how that weight is balanced between nose and tail. Again the airplane has limits ... too far forward and the airplane will nose over, too far aft and the airplane will nose up and stall. In either case, gravity will put a definite and abrupt end to your endeavor.

A missionary pilot flying from a jungle airstrip was asked to deliver an anvil to a remote post. The anvil's weight, though heavy, was within the limits for his airplane and he placed the anvil in the center of the cabin, well within the balance limits. On takeoff, he pulled back on the wheel, raising the nose gently to climb up and over the jungle canopy. The airplane lifted off the ground. But he made a fatal mistake. He had not tied the anvil down, perhaps absentmindedly assuming that the anvil was so heavy it would not move. But it did move, and when the pilot lifted the nose of the airplane as he climbed away from the ground, the airplane tilted enough so that the anvil slid toward the back of the plane, putting the airplane extremely out of balance and causing the airplane to slide tail-first back to the ground. Sadly, the pilot was killed.

Weight and balance are essential criteria in pre-flight planning.

BUT WAIT ... THERE'S MORE

We would want to know the weather along our course, as well as at our destination. It's one of the current conditions we need to know as we sit at point A. If the pilot is not "instrument rated," has not been checked and cleared by an FAA-certified flight examiner to fly solely by reference to the cockpit instruments, then it's illegal, let alone dangerous, to fly into clouds or fog, or where visibility is below certain minimums. Even an instrument-rated pilot still wants to know the weather. Thunder storms are bad for any airplane. Some private airplanes, and all commercial jets, have weather radar onboard so the pilot can see and avoid the rough patches. I saw a test plane for a certain line of business jets that had just flown through the edge of a thundercloud, a cumulonimbus, and was hammered by golf-ball-sized hail. The hail cracked the windshield and badly dented the leading edges of the wings and the nose. Most of us want to stay away from that kind of weather on the ground, let alone in a plane several thousand feet off the ground.

Then there is the route, and the knowledge of terrain. Mountains along the way require flying at certain altitudes so as not to combine sheet metal and granite in a sudden impact. Radio towers can be hard to see in daytime. The red beacon light on top is obvious at night, but not in daylight. If passengers think it would be fun to fly low to the ground while out over the prairies and plains, then the pilot had better

know in advance about radio towers, power lines and any other trap-
ish thing poking up from the ground.

What time will we fly? Night flying in a single engine aircraft
can be hair-raising over a dark forest, a large body of water or
mountainous terrain.

Flying with my friends Tim and Susie in a four-seat Cessna 172
one evening from Portland, Oregon, to a little airstrip at the town of
Joseph in the Wallowa Mountains in Northeast Oregon, the sun went
down en route, and it got dark. Crossing the Blue Mountains between
Pendleton and La Grande, I turned northward along State Highway
82 and could navigate both visually by following lights along the
road and electronically by my navigational instruments.

But when we got to Joseph, lying between rising mountain
slopes, we discovered the airstrip lights were off and no one was
available to turn them on. I circled above the town while my friend's
friend lined up his car at one end of the runway, shining his
headlights down the runway so I had a visual reference by which to
land. I allowed plenty of room for trees, which were invisible to us
at night but which we knew were there, and made a steep approach
to the airstrip, landing safely and rolling out toward the headlights of
the car. I had practiced this kind of landing many times during the
day, but when the lights are out and it's dark outside, it makes you
pay quite a bit more attention. Flying at night can be interesting.

After the planning, a pilot conducts a thorough check of the
aircraft itself. He follows a printed checklist that walks him through
every system, every moving part, and every visible section of the
airplane to make sure it's in good working order.

In school to obtain my airplane mechanic's licenses, we were told the true story about an airplane owner who left his airplane at a mechanic's shop at the airport to have the rudder worked on. The airplane owner left, and the mechanic removed the rudder from the airplane to do the repair.

At some time when the mechanic was not present, the airplane owner decided he would like to go for a little flight, so he hopped in his plane, headed for the runway and took off. And landed abruptly, shortly thereafter! I never understood how so obvious a scenario as a missing rudder could be overlooked. But it was, and it would have been as glaring as the sun in the desert if only the pilot had done his simple pre-flight check of the airplane.

Weight, balance, weather, terrain, time of day, checking the aircraft itself … all must be considered and planned for before getting into the airplane. It's all part of "where we are."

You should take no less diligence in knowing the "where we are" component in your business or in a relationship or in any venture you are going to pursue. Taking off in any way without forethought is asking for disaster. If you are going to start a small business (and "small" is where most businesses start) you need your pre-flight checklist. Know what assets and resources you have available right now, and what are the conditions of your current circumstance. Know where you are navigating from.

B: THE "WHERE YOU WANT TO BE" COMPONENT

If you have a particular destination in mind—in business, a particular net worth, for example, or a certain number of sales closed in the next twelve months, or an agenda you want to present to the state legislature so they will take action on it—then you'd better have that destination very well defined. Otherwise you will find yourself sitting on a curb somewhere (and it won't matter where) pondering Yogi Berra's enigmatic dilemma, "If you don't know where you're going, any road will get you there."

A destination is like a vision. It can give you hope, but it isn't simply hope. For one thing, hope is vague. It's real and it's valid, but it's fuzzy. Hope by itself will be a carrot forever dangling, tantalizing you and ultimately frustrating you.

A vision, on the other hand, is a picture of what you see down the road. It's where you're headed, and where you'll be if all goes according to plan. You can describe your vision in its details—its colors, its size, its sounds, its rewards. For example…

A church just starting might have a vision of reaching a thousand people in ten years. If the people and the leaders only take a "wouldn't that be nice" attitude, then no one will know where to head if ever they actually do get off the ground and start growing. The objective is more than a hope when it is expressed in specifics and when it is combined with an understanding of where they are, along with a course charted between the two points. The vision becomes something you can see in your mind and that you can describe to others in a way that enables them to see it too.

Companies sometimes print out a "Vision Statement" and post it on a wall in the lobby. This is often accompanied by a "Mission Statement." My impression of mission statements I've seen is that they are fuzzy, general and uninspiring. But a vision statement that is a picture of what the environment will look like when you get there inspires you and lets you know what things will look like when you get there.

How about this: "Our vision is to provide the customer with a great experience by offering them a fair price on a good product made by satisfied employees, and thereby gain a good return on investment for our shareholders."

That'll get you up early in the morning, won't it? That'll crank you into high gear throughout the day, right? That'll inspire you to be the best possible employee in the entire company, yes? Because ... dag-nab-bit, your adrenal glands jump into orbit over the sheer awe of such a glorious picture of a glorious future. Right?

The main thing about a good vision statement, as with the pilot's chart of his destination airport, is that you'll know when you're there. No grainy picture. Nothing out of focus. No thumb over the lens. You'll know it when you see it because you could see it before you got there.

How about this: "Our vision is to grow our market share from fifty percent to ninety-five percent in the three west coast states, to give all employees stock in the company and add shares for each year of employment, to make a profit sufficient to return a year-end bonus of ten percent of annual employee earnings to the employees, to provide a work environment where every employee has a say in its operations and helps set its annual goals, and where employees play, work and eat together like a family."

I just made that up ... no company I know actually has that vision statement. But with that kind of vision, a company and its employees know exactly where they're headed. They'll know when they arrive at their target market share; employees will know that they receive stock in the company and when; they'll know how much and when they get bonuses. And they know the journey will be fun!

NAVIGATE

A vision is a clear picture of where you're headed.

Maybe you invest in a run-down home that's been on the market for over a year because no one else could see past the stained carpets, the faded paint and the outdated kitchen. But you see what fresh paint and new carpets will do to brighten the rooms, and you see the kitchen updated with every contemporary feature you desire, and you see the yard with a healthy lawn and flowers cheering up the front porch. You see a sparkling finished product. You know what the home will look like when you finish the project.

As you stand there in the living room on the first day you see the house, you are "where you Are." As you picture in your mind what it will look like when you have finished the remodel, you are "where you want to Be.". Now the job involves planning all the steps—"the Course"—to get from here to there.

Someday I'd like to see a vision statement that reads, "We see ourselves moving from tenth in our market area to first, we see our customer base expanding from the 20-28 year-old in the Pacific Northwest region to 20-35 year-olds in all states west of the Mississippi, we see our shareholders quadrupling their investment every year - we see ourselves totally dominating!"

Domination may not be the center of your objective. Maybe for you, an objective to get up to speak in front of a Toastmasters club, or Rotary or Lions or Kiwanis, and give ten speeches in the next twelve months would be your destination. Maybe you think you'd like to live in a home on the water, or get a PhD in your field. The more clear your vision, the more likely you'll reach it simply because you know exactly where to point your nose.

BUT I'M RANDOM!

If your personality type includes the word "random," you are probably somewhat averse to defining a destination down a road you're not even sure you want to commit to in the first place. You like to keep your options open, you enjoy possibilities, and "any road will get you there" actually sounds like a great idea.

I have a solution for you that will satisfy your inclination to spur-of-the-moment planning and course changing: Just do one thing. Think through what it would look like if, after all your wandering about doing this and going there and calling someone and picking up this and … and … and, you completed just one thing. What would it be like for you to achieve just one objective, to arrive at just one destination? Of course there are other places to go, people to see, promises to keep. They will always be there. Write it all out. Put it all down on paper, in detail … just imagine any possibility that would be desirable to you and record it. Then pick one thing and do it.

Do this with one understanding: you can always change your mind. But if you do change your mind, write it down again. This way, you'll have a written destination and, if you change your mind, at least you'll know what you're changing your mind from, and at best you'll make more progress in life than you otherwise would.

For everyone else, the battle will be lethargy. Not slothfulness in working toward your destination, but laziness in not planning your destination in the first place. It will, after all take a small investment of several minutes of time. It will, most likely, require some thinking, defining and refining. And it will need to be written out. But for such a small investment up front, big progress will be made in the right direction.

C: THE COURSE FROM A TO B

By nature, your current location and your future destination are static. They are points—a place, a dot on a map, a snapshot of the circumstances of the moment and a destination somewhere down the road. The place where you are, and the place where you want to be, may be colorful, full of adjectives and adverbs and light and sound, but they are points, like the first and last frames on a movie reel.

Your course between the two, on the other hand, is dynamic. The route is motion. It may be a series of steps, or a series of individual movie frames, but all the dots and distance that connect point A to point B are the tracks you travel through time. It's the journey, the travel, the game clock, the dash between year-of-birth and year-of-death. A and B are points, C is a line—a line that may be straight, or it may be curly, but it's the connector between the points.

More than likely, your venture—or adventure or enterprise or business or any other undertaking—will not be a straight line. How many times have you set out to accomplish something, to take a hill, to write a book, to get fit, to learn a language, and continued from start to finish, non-stop, jiggle-free and stoplight-less? Is there ever a road built that has not a single bump? And if you ever do have completely smooth sailing, you won't have much of a story at the dinner table that night. Your story will not have much interest; it will not engage your listeners. The bumps along the way are what make the journey interesting. Welcome the bumps.

BUMPS

Let me brag about my first year of junior varsity wrestling as a junior at Meadowdale High School. The journey begins at point A, my first day of turnout. The destination, point B, is surviving to the end of the season. Wrestling: the toughest sport I've ever undertaken.

In between A and B, there's a Thursday, a day of challenge, when I take on the short, squat, reigning team champ in my weight class. I think of him as Short-Hulk. I am six-three and one hundred sixty pounds (at the time, I've filled out since)—a veritable and menacing beanpole whose six-foot wingspan has muscles that are, at best, visible to the unaided eye. My opponent and I are opposites as we step onto the mat. The coach blows his whistle. Short-Hulk and I meet in the middle. I grab his wrists. He grabs my wrists. I pull back. He pulls back. I pull back more. He pulls back more. I let go.

Like an old Laurel and Hardy comedy, he falls flat on his back, and I fall crossways on his chest. I am not very skillful, but Short-Hulk cannot roll away from my long, spreading wingspan. The coach is on his hands and knees, his palm checking for space under Short-Hulk's shoulders. One. Two. Three. The coach slaps the mat. We stand to our feet. The coach raises my hand … and I have qualified to wrestle in Friday night's match against Sedro Wooley High School.

But I am one pound over weight during practice, and that will disqualify me from my first-ever, inter-school wrestling match, which is tomorrow night. A major bump along the way.

How do I lose a pound in twenty-four hours when I am already the classic skin-and-bone, hit-his-growth-spurt-early sixteen-year old? I spit. I spit and spit and spit. I pass a water fountain, I spit. I step outside, I spit. I go to the boys' room, I spit. I take a shower, I spit. And I sweat. I take hot showers hoping to sweat. I put on a rubberized workout suit of pants and long-sleeved shirt and run around the track. In that non-breathing, rubberized suit, I *do* sweat. And I eat very little. In essence I both starve and dehydrate myself— a great plan just before a strenuous sports contest. Bump.

Friday night, I ride the team bus north to Sedro Wooley, and as the time passes, so does my memory of every wrestling move I have learned. My mind goes blank. This, my first ever real wrestling match, against an unknown opponent who has probably wrestled since he could toddle, and my brain does not function. So much for automatic reflex. There's no flex to re-flex! Bump.

At the Sedro Wooley boys' locker room, we dress down and take our turns in line to be weighed by the official referee. I step up and watch the referee slide the bigger weight to 100 pounds and the smaller weight to 60 pounds. I watch the pointer at the right end of the scale center at 160 pounds. Almost. Really, really close. But just a smidge over, and the pointer nudges just off center. Bump.

My coach steps in, looks at the scale, looks at the referee and says, "Well, he was right on the mark on our scale just before we left." That was true, actually.

The referee looks at my junior varsity wrestling body and no doubt figures this tall, scrawny kid will become a quick, scrawny squish on the mat, and perhaps taking pity (or enjoying the thought, it now occurs to me) he says, "Alright … get out of here."

I thank him. I dress in my wrestling tights, making me look all the more fierce … and fearsome, I'm sure. At least my legs are holding me up, which is more than I can say for my wrestling memory, which at the moment has no more hold on what to do when I take the mat than I am likely to have on my opponent when he takes me down on the mat. Bump.

Our teams sit opposite each other in cold folding chairs on either side of the mat. The half-filled gym bleachers are pulled out on our left. I scan the Sedro Wooley wrestlers. I look at our smallest wrestler in the end chair to my left—he will go first—and I count up to me. I count from the smallest wrestler on the Sedro Wooley side up to the corresponding wrestler opposite me. He looks big. Bump.

The matches start. I am not aware of who is winning or who is losing or which team is ahead or which team is behind. My brain is focused like a highway driver in a deep fog, peering intently into the very near future but not really seeing anything. My teammate next to me goes out and wrestles. I don't care. I am about to wrestle a bigger guy, in front of a live audience, half of whom will be cheering for an unknown, be-tighted scarecrow with a six-foot wingspan who at the moment sorely needs all four gifts from an Oz-ian wizard—heart, brain, courage and … a way home.

At the appointed moment, the announcer first calls for the 160-pound wrestler from Meadowdale High School. This wrestler has not eaten much, has drunk nothing and has spit and barely sweated his way past the weigh-in referee to qualify for this moment, this brief, glorious few minutes of blankness, standing in the center of a Sedro Wooley wrestling mat next to the referee, who I am sure has been looking forward to this wrestler's woeful—and speedy—demise.

The announcer calls, "Will the 160-pound wrestler from Sedro Wooley please take the mat?" I made that up. You know I have no idea what the announcer said. I am looking straight ahead to the bleachers … blank. The referee stands to my right, exactly in the center of the mat. A moment of silence. No cheers from the bleachers. "Will the 160-pound wrestler from Sedro Wooley please take the mat?" Cheerless silence.

NAVIGATE

Softly, compared to the announcer's booming microphone voice, the Sedro Wooley wrestling coach says to the referee in words that I do remember to this day, "Our wrestler did not qualify for weight."

The referee takes my right wrist. He lifts it high overhead in the glory of my victory ... and I go sit down.

I am the winner! I do not engage another wrestler that night. I do not hit the mat. I do not become a splat on the mat. I do, however, win. By default, I know ... but I am the winner!

For the rest of the season, I do not beat Short-Hulk in squad try-outs for any other inter-school matches. I compete in one, historical match between Meadowdale and Sedro Wooley. My name is not on any trophies, I set no records, I am long forgotten. But I have, under my belt, the joy of an undefeated year in wrestling. How cool is that!

There will be bumps along the way. They are almost always unavoidable. But start at point A, the first day, and head for point B in the distance. Plan your steps, and who knows ... maybe an undefeated year awaits you!

FIRST STEPS

The first and foremost reward for writing out your "where I'm going" is a sense of renewed energy and excitement. Not long ago, I had a goal of setting up my home after moving from a house with nearly three thousand square feet where two of the four bedrooms functioned as storage units (as did the garage)—to a home nearly half that size. Have you ever been so awash in details that you could not get started? I told myself that it really is simple: just open one box at a time. But when I opened that first box, there was no place to put the things I took from the box! I like the concept of "a place for

83

everything and everything in its place," it's just that I've never had a place for everything. So, for months, boxes sat unopened because, in frustration at the scope of the project, I could not work up the gumption to put on running shoes and step into the starting blocks.

Until the day my wife and my daughter-in-law went to a baby shower. I'd begun work on this book and had been hoping to find blocks of time to write. A friend suggested to me, when I whined about my plight in setting up the home and not knowing where to start, that I begin by clearing a workspace, setting up my desk and having a spot from which I could do my work. The baby shower day was my day to do that. As soon as I was alone in the house I began re-piling papers and supplies that had buried my desk, until the top of my century-old, antique "teacher's desk" was ninety percent clear. I lifted from my desktop the forty-seven inch wide brass art piece I treasured—three sailboats and a buoy on choppy water in front of a spanning bridge—and mounted it on the wall three feet above my desk.

I unplugged my laptop from its transient spot in the family room and, after an hour or so of flurry, I sat in the chair that I've enjoyed more than any other chair in my life, opened the laptop and began work in the quiet little spot I'd carved out of the chaos.

If you have ever done something like I've just described, you know the feeling I felt. In the big scheme of setting up my home, it was a very small achievement. Yet, that "one small step for a man" flipped a switch somewhere in my motivational circuitry, and I found myself more energized than a zoo at feeding time. Not only did I find myself awhir in thoughts and research and tapping the keyboard, but also I had the strongest desire to keep going on to the next step, and then the next step, and to progress toward my vision of a fully set up home with a place for everything … and storage for everything else.

The power of "first steps" is amazing. For some reason, stepping up to the plate and taking that first swing is like waking up groggy after eating too much pizza too late the night before, but knowing that somehow, sometime, the feet must hit the floor and the day must start. (When I was a kid, I found that counting down from ten, as if to launch a rocket, and predetermining that I would swing out of bed at zero, helped. I don't know why, but it helps, and I recommend you give it a try some groggy morning.)

If there's a project, an objective, a destination that seems complex and overwhelming, you must take that first step. Just as beginning one small discipline in your life will motivate you to start others, so taking the first baby step, like clearing a desk for some workspace, will energize you for the rest of it. I think it's like gravity. Gravity is such a small, simple force … yet it has power to hold the planet Neptune in orbit 2.8 billion miles from the sun.

Your first step may be a small one, but it carries a lot of weight in its effect on your motivation, your vision, and your energy. It's obvious that there are no more steps to take, no progress toward your objectives, without a first step. The significant thing is how small that first step might be for all the gravity it will supply for your ventures.

There is, of course, no point in taking steps at all unless you know where you want to go. At each of two real estate conferences I've attended, we received an assignment: write out where we wanted to be in five years. The instructions were to be as descriptive and detailed as possible so that someone else reading it could picture themselves in the scene. We were to describe a snapshot of a day five years from now, where we were, what were doing, and so on. When I finished mine I was surprised by the photographic quality of it. Though later my career changed, I can still see the scene in my mind as if a movie stopped on a single frame:

I sit on a sandy beach, soaking in the sun, smelling the fresh salt air, and enjoying the sight of my three grown kids, their spouses and my parents, all playing together by the blue water's edge. I brought them all here, a vacation week in Hawaii; I paid for a condo overlooking the breakers of the Pacific, paid for the first-class flight, paid for the meals—paid for everything, in fact, so now we enjoy our first, annual, all-family vacation. Tomorrow we fly home, first-class.

I am a healthy and fit man. Physical exercise matches mental growth, as I read a book a month.

Back home, our matching Pontiac Solstice roadster sports cars sit in the driveway of the three-thousand square-foot house I bought my wife and paid off last year. The house is on the water, where she always wanted to live, on a quiet street with a name, not a number. Our thirty-eight foot sailboat is docked nearby, not far from the airport where I've tied down my personal, home-built airplane.

My business runs smoothly, whether I'm there or not, which at the moment I'm not. I am about to live off the investments I've made, as the properties I've purchased all have positive cash flows. Book sales are brisk; speaking engagements are fun. I have no debts and I'm free to enjoy giving freely to several charitable causes.

Even though I have challenges, I face them with creativity and confidence because my outlook is as fresh as the ocean air, as uplifted as the airborne coastal birds, and as energized as the warm sun I feel on my face, here on the beach.

That's how you should see your "where you're going."

However, if a destination is the only component of your navigation, you really are in danger of just having hope. Without the "where you are" and the "how to get there," your vision will not become reality, your destination will not be reached, and your "where you want to go" will always be a nebulous sugarplum dancing in your head.

Picture that desire in your heart, that vision in your head, that sense of where it is you'd like to end up once you get there, and write it down. Clarify, be specific, and describe it with all your senses—describe it in color, describe its sounds, describe its smells, describe its lines and shapes. And head that way.

<u>Denver Approach</u>: *"Turn right to heading one-eight-zero."*
<u>Me</u>: *"One-eight-zero. Roger."*

<u>Denver Approach</u>: *"Turn left to heading one-five zero."*
<u>Me</u>: *"One-five-zero. Roger."*

<u>Direction</u>: This way. That way. And the other way.

<u>Fuel Gauges</u>: Empty.

<u>Clock</u>: Ticking.

FUMES *and a* PRAYER

Logbook

FUMES *and a* PRAYER

CHAPTER FIVE

COMMUNICATE

com-mu-ni-cate *verb* \kə-'myü-nə-,kāt\

give and receive information

FUMES *and a* PRAYER

COMMUNICATE

As I had been trained to do, the airplane was still under control. Aviate.

The obvious decision was made to land somewhere short of my intended destination at Arapahoe County Airport. Navigate.

But with Denver Approach Control not knowing my situation, they vectored me left and right like I was following an aerial cow trail. Usually, if you want to get from here to there, you decide on either the shortest route or the fastest route. In my case, flying over northern Colorado, performing a lot of lefts and rights was not in my favor as they ate up the clock ... and whatever fuel was left in the right tank.

So I did the third thing: Communicate. I got on the radio and asked Denver Approach Control, "Denver Approach, Cessna One-Zero-Six-Five-Victor. How long will you keep vectoring me around? I'm a little short on fuel."

The final three words in my transmission, "...short on fuel," raised major red flags to the air traffic controller. His response was controlled but immediate.

"Cessna Six-Five-Victor, Denver Approach. Are you declaring an emergency?"

For some reason, I hadn't expected that question. I looked at the two fuel gauges. I looked at the ground five thousand feet below. I looked at my passengers. I think an image flashed in my mind of what an emergency landing would look like—big, fluorescent yellow fire trucks, foamed runway, and lots of lights flashing—TV cameras rolling for the nightly news report.

So I responded, "No. Nope. Not yet." After all, the engine was still running, the plane was under control, and I was not panicked. Nope ... I was not declaring an emergency. I had no desire to appear, dead or alive or in any fashion, on the nightly news report.

Nevertheless, in spite of my calm and considered response, "...short on fuel" had magic, power and urgency, and Denver Approach gave me a heading straight toward Stapleton International Airport (since replaced by Denver International). Now that was what I needed—a straight line.

But Stapleton International Airport was the seventh busiest airport in the world, and I had never been there. There were six runways at Stapleton International, and since you can approach either end of a runway, you might land in any one of twelve different directions. From the air, the airport looked like a tic-tac-toe game on steroids!

Some straight-and-level time passed. My headset squawked, "Cessna Six-Five-Victor, Denver Approach. Do you have the airport in sight?" Although we were not flying in clouds, it was hazy over the city and I was not familiar with how the area looked from the air. It was difficult to see the airport.

Several minutes later, "Cessna Six-Five-Victor, Denver Approach. Do you see Runway Two-Six-Right?" I'd thought the airport was hard to see, and now the tower was asking me to identify one of twelve different runways. But the controller kept talking to me, instructing me on course correction and altitudes, encouraging me, guiding me, giving me feedback on my location and on where I was headed. We communicated.

INSTRUMENTS

The basic instruments on an airplane's instrument panel are gauges, though a pilot does not usually call them that. When a pilot gets instruction on how to fly by reference only to the instruments and not by looking outside the airplane, as when he's flying in the clouds, he is said to be "flying on instruments," not "flying on gauges." When he takes his FAA flight exam to be able to fly on instruments by himself or with passengers, without the instructor, he gets an "instrument rating," not a "gauge rating."

Instruments are one aspect of communication. Even in a car, your dashboard may indicate low oil pressure, hot water temperature, under-charging alternator, and the obvious speedometer. What these instruments give you is feedback. They tell you whether or not you're on the mark, and if you're not, they tell you how far off you are. Even a warning light has a point somewhere "off the mark," a point at which you pass the boundary of safe limits, and the little red light says, "Hey! Look at me!" They communicate like that.

Aircraft instruments have needles—or they have an outline of an airplane—over a background which has increments indicating altitude, airspeed, rate of climb, degree of bank in a turn, compass direction and more. Airline manufacturers today equip instrument panels with "glass". Many small, private planes today come equipped with a "glass cockpit." A glass cockpit replaces traditional, mechanical instruments with monitors—screens that display the same information but in a compact and selectable way. The pilot or co-pilot views flight gauges, navigation instruments and warning lights on these screens.

In the "olden" days, the instrument panel held round, square and rectangular instruments. Cessna N1065V was built in 1974 and had the older style instruments. They're not as snazzy as an instrument panel that looks like the space shuttle, but they work quite well; and besides, there weren't any glass cockpits when Six-Five-Victor was built.

The basic instruments tell the pilot how fast he is going, how high he is, how fast he's climbing or descending, how much bank he has while making turns. There is usually a vertical stack of radio and navigational units mounted in the middle of the instrument panel for talking to air traffic controllers and to tower personnel, and for tuning in to navigational transmissions from sites along his route. In both digital and mechanical displays, there are needles to indicate the appropriate information to the pilot.

In 1937 the Royal Air Force determined which flight instruments were the most essential. Today every pilot is taught to scan the "T" which was the normal configuration of four of the six basic flight instruments. At the top center is the attitude indicator, also called the artificial horizon, with a background that shows brown for the ground and blue for the sky, divided by a black line that represents the horizon. In the foreground is a stick-figure airplane representing the plane itself as viewed from behind—looking forward. This instrument tells you the "attitude" of the airplane—its position relative to the horizon. You can tell at a glance if your wings are level and if you are climbing, gliding or turning. The attitude indicator is usually the most oft referred to instrument in a pilot's scan.

To the left of the attitude indicator is the airspeed indicator and to the right is the altimeter. Below the attitude indicator, at the bottom of the "T," is a heading indicator which is a gyroscopically stabilized compass. The other two basic flight instruments are the turn-and-bank indicator and the rate-of-climb indicator showing, in hundreds of feet per minute, how fast the airplane is climbing or descending. These are to the left and right of the base of the "T."

CHASING THE NEEDLES

Responding to the feedback your instruments give you can be a challenge. There's a common tendency among newer pilots to "chase the needles" when they learn to fly on instruments. Let's say you're the pilot and you want to fly at an altitude of 9,000 feet above sea level. You level off as the needles on your altimeter indicate 9,000 feet. Invariably, air currents and undetectable movements of the controls will move the airplane up or down a bit even in fairly smooth air. When this happens, the needles on the altimeter indicate that you are above your desired altitude, or below it. This is similar to driving your car down the freeway. You don't drive the car straight down the road without the car straying from its course. You must make constant minor corrections with the steering wheel.

As a new pilot flying on instruments you might notice a change of altitude and make the appropriate correction. If the airplane has lost a little altitude, you pull back on the control yoke or stick which pulls the airplane nose up and you climb back to 9,000 feet. If the airplane has gone above your desired altitude, you push on the yoke or stick to push the nose down so you descend back to 9,000 feet.

The problem you will have is called "chasing the needles." It usually takes just a little pressure on the controls to make the correction and get back to 9,000 feet. But "chasing the needles" means that when just a little correction is needed, or when the difference between where you are and where you want to be is so small that you really don't need to bother at all, you make corrections you may not need to make at all.

Say you're a touch below your 9,000 feet. You pull back on the controls, watch the needles on the altimeter reach 9,000 feet, level off, but now you've climbed up past 9,000 feet. You are above your altitude, so you push on the controls to get back down to 9,000 feet, chasing the needles, and as they reach 9,000 feet you level off, but you descend through 9,000 feet. Now you are below your altitude, so you pull back again, chase the needles, climb above your altitude, make your correction, chase the needles, descend too far, climb again, chase the needles.......

And that's just the altimeter. Throw in the airspeed indicator, rate-of-climb indicator, turn-and-bank indicator, heading indicator and, if you are prone to chasing the needles, you can have quite a roller coaster ride indeed. If you have passengers, you'd probably better provide them with "sick sacks."

Ups and downs happen. There are very few flying days that are completely as smooth as silk. Most times you will feel normal bumps as you fly through the fluid currents of air.

There are acceptable limits of variation—how far you can vary from an exact course. If you are close, and still headed in the right direction, it may be best just to leave things alone as long as your conditions remain near to what you want them to be.

COMMUNICATE

The purpose of instruments is to give you feedback. The pilot doesn't tell the instruments what to do, the instruments tell the pilot where he is, and the pilot makes the correlation between that information and his plans to get from where he is to where he wants to go. Instruments, therefore, are for communication to the pilot.

If you are preparing for a flight, you do need to give the instruments some input such as the altimeter setting at the airport (barometric pressure reading) and the radio frequencies of navigational systems you'll be connecting with, but from then on, your instruments are giving you feedback. You know the direction you want to fly and the compass tells you if you're on course or not and, if not, how far off course you are. You know the altitude you want to fly at and the altimeter tells you that you are there or, again, if you are too high or too low and by how many feet. You know how fast you want to fly and the airspeed indicator tells you how fast you are flying—if it says you're going slower than desired, you can make the appropriate throttle adjustments.

The important thing here seems obvious perhaps, that it is you telling the airplane where you are, where you want to go, and how you desire to get there. That's your job. The instruments' job is to tell you how you're doing in your venture. "Hey! You're a little to the north of where you want to be." Or, "At this speed, you'll be landing way too fast!" Or, "You're pulling two Gs—really? Are you sure you want to be turning this steeply?"

The point of having instruments is to monitor how you *are* doing in relation to how you *want* to be doing. You have to decide what direction you want to head, how fast you want to climb or descend, what altitude you want to fly at, how fast you want your engine to run, when you want to turn and how steep you want to make that turn. All the instruments do is give you feedback.

EMOTIONAL INVOLVEMENT

Many years ago I explained to an acquaintance a problem I had at the time. He listened for a few minutes and then he said something that was both clear and simple. I was struck by the common sense and said something like, "How come I didn't think of that!" He replied, "All you needed was to talk to someone who wasn't emotionally involved." Today I've forgotten both my problem and his solution, but I will never forget the principle he gave me about the value of feedback from someone who is not emotionally involved.

That is not to say that you shouldn't listen to friends or to family or to your spouse. Their input is valuable in that they most likely know you well, know your weaknesses and blind spots, and their words of wisdom can be aimed right at the bullseye, at least as they see it.

If they are emotionally involved, however, their vision may be as clouded as yours. Their confidence may be even lower, their advice directed more at self-preservation or at applying a bandaid than in seeing a big picture and offering un-panicked guidance. Further, being emotionally involved often means people see what they want to see and, perhaps worse, say what they think you want to hear.

Hans Christian Andersen's short story, *The Emperor's New Clothes*, illustrates the tendency to say what we think someone wants us to say whether or not it represents the whole truth. In the story, the emperor loves clothes to the extent that he puts on new garb every hour of the day. Then The Unexpected happens. Two swindlers approach the emperor with the promise of such finely made clothes that he will not even feel the weight of them and that the exquisite new clothes will even have the power to reveal those who are stupid or incompetent because to such people these fine clothes will be invisible. When the emperor sends his minister to check on the "tailors," the minister can't see anything he's shown because in truth there's nothing to see. Yet, afraid of being judged stupid or incompetent, he reports to the emperor that the fabric is indeed marvelous, which is exactly what he knows the emperor wants to hear. The emperor himself cannot see the clothes when the swindlers dress him and, when he parades in front of the crowds to show off his new clothes, no one on the streets sees any clothes either.

But they are afraid to say so. They are emotionally involved. Each person fears for their reputation and, against their reason, proclaim the magnificence of the emperor's new clothes. That is, until a boy, unconcerned with such things as stupidity or incompetence, says it like it is ... the emperor has no clothes! The boy has no emotional involvement in the whole affair, he has nothing to gain, nothing to lose, no fears. Unattached emotionally, the boy is the one figure who is able to see things as they actually are and to guide everyone back to the truth.

TUNNEL VISION

Our problem lies in the proverbial forest and trees scenario. Most often, when you face something unexpected, your vision narrows to your immediate surroundings, your focus becomes near sighted, you can feel almost claustrophobic. You develop myopic tunnel-vision. In other words, all you see are trees, and even then it's just the trees immediately in front of you.

Flying on fumes and a prayer tends to cause everything outside the airplane to disappear, to cease to exist. As in moderate to severe hypothermia where the lifeblood of your body is forced away from surface blood vessels to focus on the vital organs, so when you are blindsided your mental and emotional resources surge to the core concern. Your emotional reaction at the time helps you survive but gives you tunnel vision in the process and does nothing to keep you on track or even to recognize that there is a track to be on.

Someone who is not emotionally involved is not hindered by such blinders. Like a fire lookout atop a mountain ridge, they see the entire forest. They see where you are, they see where you want to go, and they see the best way for you to get there. An ability to see both forest and trees means you won't have to wander through the woods hoping that blind luck will get you back on the road to your objective.

The order is important. Aviate makes it possible to Navigate safely. Navigate provides a plan, the departure, destination and course, which is essential information for the person with whom you'll Communicate. Aviate and Navigate tells the person giving you feedback that you're under control and ready for the feedback they'll give you.

The reason Communicate is third, after Aviate and Navigate, is that the one who is offering you guidance needs to know first that you do have control of the basics (otherwise you're going to crash anyway) and second that you know where you are, what assets and resources you have available, where you want to be when it's all over, and what steps you see yourself taking to get there. So you must first Aviate, then Navigate and finally Communicate ... in that order.

COMMUNICATE

AFTER HELLO

What do you need to communicate? A basic radio communication from a pilot who intends to land at a municipal airport might sound something like this:

"Blogginsville Tower, Cessna One-Zero-Six-Five-Victor, ten miles south of airport, for landing, with Information Tango."

In that brief transmission, the pilot informs the air traffic controller in the tower who it is that's calling (the identify of his aircraft), the current location of the pilot (ten miles south), where the pilot wants to end up (on the ground at the airport), and what information the pilot already has (Information Tango, recorded information that conveys wind, weather and visibility at the airport so the controller doesn't have to repeat it to every aircraft in the area). The tower will acknowledge with further instructions, "Cessna Six-Five-Victor, Blogginsville Tower, proceed inbound and notify tower when five miles out. Be aware of two other aircraft in the pattern."

The exchange implies that the airplane is under control, and Aviate is covered. The pilot informs the tower of his current position and his desired landing spot, and Navigate is covered. The pilot expects the tower to respond with any instructions or information that will help him on the journey, and Communicate is covered.

What if you've been hit hard by an unexpected event in your business? You call a consultant from outside your company. An outside business consultant gets the details of your immediate circumstances, gets from you an analysis of your current assets and resources relevant to the immediate issues including perhaps your balance sheet and cash flow statements, your receivables, your personnel, your location ... anything you've got going for you at the moment. In other words, you give your consultant a clear picture of where you are, then provide another picture of what it will look like when you get to where you want to go. Your consultant can help you with this by asking probing questions, but you'll need to fill in the blanks ... it's your vision, not theirs. Then you'll define the specific steps to take to get from here to there. A Gap Analysis describes what lies between your current position and your desired position.

Problem solving, a search for what went wrong, can happen after this, but first you'll need to Aviate, Navigate and Communicate. If you don't, you can end up searching manuals, flipping this and that switch, and racking your brain all the way into the ground. After you've got control of the basics, after you have a picture of where you are and where you want to go and after you're talking with a consultant or coach, *then* find out what caused the problem so you know what not to do next time. (The best key I know of in discovering what caused a problem is to look for what changed. Find that, and you'll often find the problem.)

But first: Aviate, Navigate, Communicate.

SPEAKING OF SPEAKING

A public speaker told me he gave what he thought was a winning speech. It had great content and he delivered it well. He had already given over 150 speeches. Nevertheless, he was humbled by a response to this speech that said he seemed overly nervous and that he spoke with a staccato-like style. His focus turned from the message he was trying to deliver to the details of how his voice sounded and what activities he should or should not do before making his presentation. He saw the trees, but not the forest.

A speaking coach will help him look first at the basics of his presentation—audience-appropriate content, internal structure and flow, posture and breathing from his diaphragm. The coach looks for humor, an engaging opening, captivating stories and a point the audience can take away. These are basics.

Then the coach will look at what resources the speaker currently has. Perhaps the speaker has lots of experience, a radio-quality voice, an ability to project, a physical and commanding presence, and so on. The coach discovers where the speaker wants to be, which might include being less nervous, telling better stories, getting more laughs, getting paid more. Finally, steps are planned that will take the speaker on the journey to his dream.

Here, as always, Communicate should take place with someone not emotionally involved. A speaker's primary coach should not be their spouse. A speech, carefully crafted, painstakingly practiced and daringly delivered becomes his baby. There's way too much at stake in the spousal relationship to risk messing with this baby, and any feedback from someone who feels the baby is also theirs is likely to be either too easy or too harsh. Getting feedback from your spouse is necessary, of course, and probably inevitable. But it isn't coaching. The kind of coaching that will be most helpful comes from someone not emotionally involved.

THE LONE RANGER

The Lone Ranger was a lone ranger, but he was not an *a*lone ranger. He was called a lone ranger because he worked alone, apart from other rangers—an early episode explained how everyone thought the character named Reid, who became The Lone Ranger, was killed along with five other Texas Rangers in an ambush. He became effective because no one knew who he was; and the person he really was, they thought was dead.

But The Lone Ranger wasn't alone. He had Tonto, his sidekick and companion who shared the adventures, who gave feedback and who sometimes saved the day. No doubt, The Lone Ranger would have had fewer televised adventures and fewer comic books on the shelves if Tonto had not been there helping chase the bad guys, pursuing opportunities, and sharing the dangers and the credit. In many episodes, it's likely The Lone Ranger would not have survived the challenges, would not have ridden off into the sunset with a hearty "Hi-ho, Silver. Away!" without what Tonto gave him—an extra pair of eyes, and someone to offer feedback.

I like the word, "ranger." It speaks of journeys, of dangers, of challenges, of discoveries. It's a word in motion. Like the original Ford Mustang just looking like it was going somewhere, a "ranger" is someone on the move, out on the range, traveling in wide open spaces. A ranger is not a wanderer; a ranger is on a mission, traveling a certain area with a clear purpose. But it can get pretty lonely out there if you are a *lone* ranger.

There are those brave souls, rangers if you will, who take on great adventures alone. Mount Everest has been climbed solo. Fifteen year-olds have sailed around the world solo. I flew the pattern at the La Grande airport solo.

Yet even these adventurers were in contact with someone ... at least by radio. All had maps and charts, they had the accounts of those who had gone before, and they had people following their progress. Seldom is any venture truly done alone, without communication of any sort.

COMMUNICATE

Think of the movies you have seen, the stories you know. How many of them are about a solo venture? Not many. They usually come in pairs: Butch Cassidy and the Sundance Kid, Indiana Jones and Marion, Batman and Robin, Bonnie and Clyde, Abbot and Costello, Laurel and Hardy, Tom and Jerry. Sometimes there are small groups: *The Magnificent Seven, Hogan's Heroes, Saving Private Ryan*. The point is that these pairs and groups are not just traveling through their adventures in silence. They talk! They communicate. They provide each other constant input and feedback, continual checks and balances, convivial encouragement and reinforcement.

Some of us on the planet do have something of an independent spirit. We don't need someone telling us why we shouldn't do something or what can go wrong if we do. We know where we are, we see where we want to be, and we set our course to get from here to there. And yet, my experience is that most journeys are best tackled with companionship, with others who, shoulder-to-shoulder, share the tasks, share the trip, share the triumph. We simply enjoy someone to talk to.

A sightseeing trek to the golden shores of Wagga-Wagga Land will most likely be more pleasurable in the company of good friends to talk with. But when The Unexpected happens, having someone to talk to can be crucial to your survival, let alone your success.

When life hits its bumps, it can send you flying head over heels where you don't know which way is up or if there even is an "up" anymore. Sometimes you find yourself buried so deep the weight is crushing. Sometimes it's so dark you must stand still or risk bumping into a chair or, worse, falling into an invisible abyss. Sometimes you just run out of gas. Sometimes life is like that, isn't it?

Sometimes you have everything under control, you understand the basics and are doing them. You know what is at the core of your endeavor and you are sticking to it. Sometimes you know exactly where you are, you see clearly where you want to be, and you have a well thought-through course to follow and you're on course. But sometimes The Unexpected jumps out at you, throws a bump in the road and shakes you to your bones. You had it right: Aviate and Navigate. Now it is essential that you Communicate.

"BASIC" COMMUNICATION

I hit a bump once at Basic Training. My group had been shown the obstacle course the day before and now, supposedly familiar with it, we climbed the ropes, jumped through hoops, crawled through chicken wire tunnels with bangs and explosions that simulated mine fields and pulled ourselves along ropes stretched over long water traps. When we got near the end, we came to the rope swing, a pool of water about twenty feet across that could be crossed (going around would get you "shot," I suppose) only by grabbing a rope suspended about twenty feet off the ground and swinging Tarzan-style across the pond.

I don't know who does this in real life, or in combat, but in Basic Training you don't really want to ask too many questions. I'd already been threatened in the chow hall by the Training Instructor (modern equivalent of the old Drill Sergeant) on my first night at Basic. Nose-to-nose (I was so excited ... it was just like in the movies!) this very large, very muscular, very scary sergeant asked me very impolitely if I would like to have my face rubbed down the salad bar. No one came up to tell him he was out of line, so I quietly responded with the only thing I could think of, a modest and appropriate, "No, sir." There were other questions he asked, but all I remember from the episode now is my series of responses … "Yes, sir." "No, sir." "Yes, sir." "No, sir." Apparently I passed his test, as I left the chow hall with a salad-free face. At some level, I decided, we had communicated!

An unfamiliar sergeant stood at the top of a little knoll just to the left of the rope swing. I had done fairly well, I was surprised to see, as my six-foot, three, somewhat more muscular body had got me to the rope swing in third place, not that it was a race … but I did notice. There was a gentleman standing on our right, next to the edge of the water, holding a long pole with a hook in its end. His job was to reach the hanging rope using the pole and hook and get the rope into the hands of the first man in line.

That being done, Number One swung across, landed on the far side, and without looking back released the rope … just let it go. The rope did not swing back far enough for Number Two, who was right in front of me, to reach out and catch it, so he looked at the gentleman with the long pole who obliged him by hooking the rope and passing it to him. Number Two grabbed the rope, swung out, and he too reached the far side. And he too let go of the rope without looking back. As before, the rope did not swing back far enough for even my six-foot wing span to reach it, so I did what Number Two had done. I looked at the gentleman standing by the pool.

At this point, I hit a bump in life. The Unexpected appeared. I heard a voice. Now, sometimes there are voices you just don't hear. Other times there are voices you hear but you ignore. Then there are voices you hear and you'd better pay attention because if you don't there will be a price to pay. One of those voices you want to pay attention to is the voice of your Training Instructor at Basic Training.

I give that sergeant at the top of the knoll full marks for his ability to Communicate.

I looked at the gentleman on my right, waiting for him to reach out with his long pole, hook the rope and hand it to me. But he didn't. He didn't do anything. He didn't say anything. He just stood there. At the same time the voice of the sergeant at the top of the knoll rang out, "That's your rope, son!" Good: Clear feedback! Excellent: Communication! I should have taken immediate action. But I didn't. I looked at the gentleman with the long pole. The rope swung back across a ways, then pendulumed back towards me, but this time not even as close as when Number Two first let it go.

I turned to look at the sergeant at the top of the knoll and hollered back, "But he didn't let it go right!" In hindsight, that was not a brilliant thing to say … but hey! … we were simulating combat … sort of … right? I was under duress. Sometimes you say things under duress that you later regret.

He squared up at me and hollered right back, only louder, "I didn't ask if he let it go right. I said, 'It's your rope, son!'" OK. Got it. Now we've really Communicated! I understand the basics of the situation … maybe that's why they call it Basic Training. I also know exactly where I am, and I have a clear picture of where I want to be. I didn't know Aviate, Navigate, Communicate yet, but it was all right there, in that moment, standing at the edge of the water, looking at a rope which was now on its way back toward me for the third time. But its swing was dying.

Though the rope was slow and out of reach, I heeded the words of the sergeant at the top of the knoll. I crouched down low, just as I had when my mom checked me off in my Cub Scout handbook the day she watched me crouch and jump out of the way of an imaginary bear … jump left, jump right … jump straight up and out for the rope in a flying leap that ought to have impressed the sergeant at the top of the knoll, as well as the gentleman with the long pole, as well as the next man, Number Four. With perfect aim, my hands grabbed the rope, gripped tightly, and though low enough on the rope that my right boot dragged through the water and half filled it, I still grabbed high enough on the rope so that my feet just made it to the edge on the far side where I arched my back, bent my knees and let inertia carry me forward to the grass beyond the pond.

I don't know what I would have done without that sergeant at the top of the knoll who could see where I was, knew where I wanted to be, and knew exactly how I was to get there. All because when I hit a bump in the road that day, when The Unexpected happened on the obstacle course, there was this one thing to encourage me across: Communicate.

I hope that my story, which actually happened, will help you when the really serious bumps of life happen. I've had a few of those too.

I got kicked out of college for bad grades. I got kicked out of a second college for ethical failure. I went through a divorce. I had a business fail, and then owed tens of thousands of dollars.

I spent a week in the hospital with autoimmune hemolytic anemia, where my white blood cells were playing Pac-Man with my red blood cells, chomping them to bits so that if my red blood cell count had gone any lower, my body, my very swollen liver and my life would have been in very serious danger.

I stood by my mom as she lost her third battle with cancer, and I watched her take her last breath and die ... perhaps the most poignant moment of my life.

None of these things were expected. All of them were quite serious. And I know that you too have had your bumps in the road, and very likely will have more. That's why it's good to be prepared with these concepts of Aviate, Navigate, Communicate. You will need a firm grip on the basics. You will need to know where you are, where you want to be and the course you'll take between the two. And you will need someone not emotionally involved to talk to, someone who knows where you are, who knows where you want to go, and who can give you feedback, direction and encouragement.

RELIABILITY

I've made the case for communicating with someone not emotionally involved so that you get fair, reasoned and unbiased feedback and advice. There is one more quality that you must have in the one with whom you communicate when The Unexpected happens. You must communicate with someone reliable.

Go to the local bar, toss back a few and share your woes with Joe Bloggins, who sits next to you and whom you just met thirty minutes earlier and who has also tossed back a few, listen to Joe's advice … and you might as well open fortune cookies for your life's direction. Please don't go there. Don't do that. Not when you need to know how to handle real life hurts and surprises, not when disaster hits you hard, head on, and you know you're going down.

Joe Bloggins, sitting next to you on a bar stool, fits the criteria of being unemotionally involved. He doesn't even know you. But he is most likely not reliable. And even if he is, how would you know that?

COMMUNICATE

As a senior at Lakes High School in Lakewood, Washington—I moved to Lakewood halfway through my junior year, just after I became an undefeated wrestler—I was near my first love, the mountains. The entrance to Mount Rainier National Park was only fifty miles away, an hour's drive, then another hour up winding roads to Paradise, a major tourist site right at timberline on the south side of the mountain. I wanted badly to climb Mount Rainier, I talked about it, I read books about it, I spoke with those who had done it.

One day a new friend (having only been there a few months, all friends were new) sat with me in the cafeteria. Striking up a conversation was easy and when he discovered my interest in mountaineering, he began to tell me his stories. Day after day he added bits of information, exciting little tales of his adventures with the guide service. He told me about the requirements I would need to meet to do what he did. He told about how much oxygen I needed to be able to take in, measured by chest expansion as I inhaled.

He knew where I was and where I wanted to be. And he was telling me how to get there and encouraging me with the possibility that I too could do what he did. Yes! I could see me doing it!

This went on every day for three weeks. Something about that oxygen thing, though, got me thinking. The figures he gave me for the required chest expansion were remarkable and made me squinch my eyebrows down and squint my eyes as I looked at my own chest to see how much it expanded when I breathed in. Try it. It doesn't expand all that much. And that got me to wondering. At lunch, I asked him about that. Did I have the measurement right? Really? That much? Unbelievable.

A couple other little factoids later and my suspicions grew. I confronted him with some inconsistencies. And then he confessed: He had made the whole thing up. The whole thing! He had not one second of experience, he had not one piece of equipment, and he probably had very little chest expansion! He thought it was funny. "Wasn't that fun?" he asked. No, it wasn't. "Haven't you ever done that? Haven't you ever played along with somebody and made it up as you went?" he asked with a smile. No, I hadn't. He made it sound like he did this all the time, that other people did it as well, and that it was a normal form of entertainment.

To this day, I think I have a little trouble with trust, because one time in high school I went into Communicate mode with someone who was unreliable. Today my modus operandi is, to quote Ronald Reagan, "trust, but verify."

That's a good idea—trust, but verify—especially when the ventures you pursue are serious, when they are meaningful to you, when you sink your heart and soul into them, when they matter. I trust that the air traffic controller on the other end of our radio link is qualified—he is not emotional about my situation, and he is reliable. I trust that the pastor with whom I share my challenges and shortcomings is qualified and reliable. I trust that the life coach I meet with is unemotionally involved, that she will give me unfiltered advice, that she understands where I am and where I want to be, that the training she's received and the experience she's gained will ensure her reliability.

Don't go to Joe Bloggins at the bar unless you just need to chill, if you just need to get things off your chest, but don't expect anything more than a listening ear. *Do* expect that anything you say to him *will* be repeated elsewhere.

Go to someone not emotionally attached to you or your situation, someone with reliable credentials and experience. When you're hit by The Unexpected, go to that person when you need: Communicate.

You might be a lone ranger, but don't be an *a*lone ranger.

FUMES *and a* PRAYER

Logbook

FUMES *and a* PRAYER

CHAPTER SIX

PREDICTABILITY:
Thinking Past the End of Your Nose

pre·dict verb \pri-'dikt\

foretell something

PREDICTABILITY

I live in the Pacific Northwest, specifically in the Puget Sound area. If you think weather predicting is an inexact science, you should live here! It's amazing to me that with modern satellite telemetry scoping out the whole planet, our ability to predict rain is still shaky. One study revealed that TV station weather reports were accurate 85 percent of the time regarding rain the next day, but right only 73 percent of the time on the seven-day outlook.

Why can't meteorologists look at satellite data, observe the high pressure areas, the low pressure areas, the flow of the jet stream, the lay of the land, the direction of wind, the level of humidity, and be nearly 100% correct in telling me whether or not it will rain this week which, where I live, it does 158 days out of the year anyway? If you predicted every day that it would rain tomorrow in Seattle, you would be correct nearly half the time!

How good are we, really, at predicting the outcome of life's adventures if we can't even say with a great degree of probability whether or not we'll need our umbrella or our sunglasses tomorrow?

It doesn't take much observation to notice (if not understand) that the world is full of variables. This is the nature of our concept of "The Unexpected." The ability to predict is, of course, essential to making any kind of progress at all. If we were unable to predict at all, we would live either in confusion or paralysis. Why open the refrigerator unless there's a good probability that there's food in it?

Why get out of bed in the morning unless you're pretty sure you'll stand vertically and that gravity will hold your feet to the floor? Why start a business without a prediction, in your own mind at least, that you will prosper from it? Why drive the airplane down the runway without a sense of assurance that, at the right speed, the wings will lift you off the runway? To predict something is to be reasonably sure of an outcome.

If we were unable to predict, there could be no trust. It's as simple as predicting that the office chair I'm about to sit in, which has always supported me in the past and which still seems to be holding together as it was designed to do, will do the same for me now and, most likely, tomorrow too.

The kicker is that what we predict, what we see as probable, is not infallible. There are always variables. The law of gravity apparently applies to the entire universe. Without it, your world would literally be upside down. It is a universal law of physics. And yet—using other laws of physics, the law of gravity can be overcome.

OVERCOMING GRAVITY

In 1738, Daniel Bernoulli published his discovery that the faster a fluid flows (including air, which acts like a fluid) the lower its pressure at a given point. Bernoulli's Principle had a lot to do with the development of flight.

Have you ever looked at an airplane's wing? Did you notice that the upper surface of the wing is more curved than the lower surface? If you take a tape measure and check the length from the front of the wing, its leading edge, over the top, to the trailing edge, you will find that it is longer than if you measure from the front to the back underneath the wing.

Picture that wing flying straight into the air—even if the air is still, the movement of the wing through the air at a speed, say, of one hundred twenty miles an hour, creates in effect a wind that the wing flies through. Since the measurement over the top of the wing is longer than the measurement under the wing, the wind must travel faster over the top than it does under the wing. And Bernoulli showed that the faster a fluid flows, the lower its pressure.

As it affects a wing, that means there is more air pressure under the wing than over it, and the wing is "sucked" skyward, lifted into the lower pressure—with apologies to the technically inclined for the terminology. Thus the principle of lift does not do away with the law of gravity, but it does overcome its power.

The law of gravity is not infallible in that sense. So when I walk out to the airplane, it is sitting there on the tarmac because the law of gravity predictably holds it there. And if I do nothing with it (and if security at the airport is adequate) I can predict that the airplane will still be there on the ground tomorrow.

But if I preflight the airplane, run up the engine, taxi to the runway and gather speed down the runway, I'm reasonably sure that we can use other laws of physics to get the airplane off the ground. These laws are predictable, and yet we make use of their subjectiveness to variables.

TAKE ACTION

Grasping the concepts of Aviate, Navigate, Communicate implies that you have the capacity to think ahead, to imagine a desirable outcome, to set a course—and to reasonably predict the outcome. Equally, you are able to recognize and respond to changes that occur, to allow for variables to occur and to react appropriately for the good of everyone involved. To consider what the basics are in any venture or situation assumes that you will take action on those elements you decide are basic.

If the basics of good health are eating right, exercising and getting enough rest, then it's not enough just to know these things ... you must act on what you know and actually eat right, actually get the exercise and actually go to bed on time. Doing these things makes it probable that good health will be the result.

REALITY

Someone once told me to take a reality pill. I suppose I was, at that moment, too far into dreams and visions and positive thinking. There must be a balance, a recognition that life is made up both of dreams and of reality—that sometimes you reach objectives and sometimes you don't. I'm a believer in reaching for your dreams as if they *will* become reality, but only a fool believes everything they can visualize will come true. Consider two professional football teams in a crucial, season-deciding game. Both teams visualize the desired outcome, and pundits predict winners; both teams can taste victory; both teams point to God when they score a touchdown. But only one of the teams will win and the other will lose. That's life. That's reality.

Is it possible to be blindsided and not recover, in spite of doing everything you know to do? Of course. My mother fought cancer three times in her life. She fought bravely, she fought well, yet after two years in her third battle, she lost the fight. On her last day, having sipped a few drops of water from a spoon in the morning and having the smallest bite of jello, she spent the rest of the day in a coma. Dad called me midday and said I should probably come over to the house because the hospice nurse said she probably wouldn't make it through the night. It struck me that I had been with her the day I was born ... and now I was at her bedside when, just after midnight, she took her last breath, exhaled, and died.

I have conducted funerals, and this surety is always clear for each one of those present ... life has an end. We face our own mortality at a funeral. It is a certainty of life that it began on a certain date and that it will end on a certain date. Most grave markers exhibit the date of birth and the date of death. While we might be able to prolong that second date by paying attention to our health, it is inevitable that one day we will be blindsided for the final time.

Much has been made of that gravestone and the dash between the dates. That dash represents all the life that happens between birth and death. And that's the focus of Aviate—Navigate—Communicate. One day at a time, laying a foundation of basic elements of your venture. One day at a time, taking a picture of your current assets and resources, sketching out the details of the picture you want to see down the road and planning each step to get from here to there, and then, one day at a time, taking those steps. One day at a time, sharing your situation and your vision and receiving feedback to increase your wisdom and strength for the journey.

The better your information, the greater will be your ability to predict the outcome you desire. The strength of your predictions, based on solid information, determines the probability of those outcomes—that is, the better your chances of success. The surer you are that you have the basics correctly identified and the stronger you are in obeying the requirements of those basics, the better able you will be to handle the variables that invariably find you like a shark drawn to blood.

WORKAROUNDS

I'm sure you know people who run into a wall and just give up right there. I just don't get that. Sometimes people look for open doors, and if there aren't any they say it must not be God's will. My friend David told me once that in situations where he set an objective and then ran into an obstacle, he always looked for a way around it. I like David's approach. He said if the door was closed, he knocked on it. If it didn't open, he knocked harder and louder. If it didn't open, he tried the handle. If it still didn't open, he looked for a key. If he didn't find a key, he picked the lock. If he couldn't pick the lock, he took the hinges off the door. If the door didn't come off, he looked for a window to climb through. If, after all that, he still couldn't get through the wall, then he might start to consider the possibility that there might be some chance that God might have a different door for him. That's a great way to handle life when variables get in the way of your predictions.

Two days before Chuck Yeager made his historic flight in the Bell X-1, he fell while horseback riding and broke two ribs. If he had told the doctors about it, he might have been grounded and someone else might have gone down in history on that day for being the first to fly faster than the speed of sound. But he didn't tell anyone except Jack Ridley, his engineer and project manager, about his injury. He had his side taped up by a veterinarian in a nearby town.

PREDICTABILITY

Yeager had flown the X-1 eleven times already, three times in non-powered glides followed by eight powered flights. He had grown up around farm machinery, and had spent hundreds of hours in flying machines, so that he knew and understood mechanical systems as thoroughly as any pilot could. His eyesight was 20-15 in each eye. In other words, he was prepared. He had a grasp of the basics; he knew where the flight test program was at the moment, and he knew where they wanted it to go. He had survived the "attack" of a variety of unexpected situations ... smoke filled cockpits, complete electrical failures, nearly uncontrollable spins following engine failures. He talked it over with Ridley. And he believed he could do this.

The Bell X-1 was carried to 8,000 feet under the wing of a B-29., attached by a shackle that formerly gripped bombs. The Bell X-1 pilot was lowered down through the bomb bay in the belly of the B-29 to the opened hatch of the X-1. Once inside the X-1, the test pilot ordinarily closed the cockpit hatch with his right hand and proceeded with preflight activities prior to release and self-sustained flight.

But with The Unexpected broken ribs, Yeager knew he would not be able to reach up and close the hatch, and the latch was impossible to reach by any of the flight crew from the B-29. Yeager adapted to the bump in his plans by doing two things. First, he communicated his plight to one person, but not just any person. He did not share anything about the broken ribs to the doctors. Rather, he shared the predicament with Ridley, the one person who knew Yeager, knew his abilities and his determination better than anyone else did—someone who would help him, not ground him.

Second, they devised a practical plan to deal with The Unexpected broken ribs and to enable Yeager to close the hatch. You would think that the pair would come up with some engineering marvel, perhaps wiring a system to operate pulleys or levers or pistons that would close the hatch. But the marvel they came up with was a broomstick handle. In a corner of the hangar was a broom with a wooden handle. Ridley sawed off about ten inches of the end of the broomstick and offered it to Yeager whose useless right arm could not reach the latch. When the plane reached an altitude of 8,000 feet, Yeager, awkward and in pain, climbed aboard the X-1, grasped the broomstick handle and with his left hand leveraged the hatch shut. And that day Chuck Yeager flew into history.

THE VALUE OF VARIABLES

The things of life are not very predictable. How do you handle glitches in your plans? What do you do when fuel runs unexpectedly low and you find yourself praying your way to a gas station? What do you do when an unexpected bill arrives in the mail? What do you do when a child grows and decides to test their wings in a way you hadn't planned on? What do you do when you lose your house in foreclosure? What do you do when your marriage falls apart? What do you do when you are suddenly laid off after years of service to your company?

As certain as you are of your predictions and the probability of your success, it doesn't take a long look at history, or even last week, to be as equally certain that variables will be encountered along the way. I am convinced that it's the unpredictability of life—those moments when variables hit, those unexpected happenstances, the time when choices are made, when reactions take place, when experience, knowledge and wisdom are demanded and tested—it is in those moments where life happens. It is right there that our stories are made. Those are the events that reveal what we're made of, mold us into maturity and leave a legacy ... an inheritance to pass on to those who follow. That is the value of the unpredictability of life.

There've been times, haven't there, where you've been sailing along smoothly, predictably ... then been hit by an unforeseen gust that threatens to knock you over? Lake Pend Oreille, Idaho's largest lake at sixty-five miles long, nestles in the Rockies between four mountain ranges. Sailing on the lake challenges a sailor's skills because winds descending onto the lake from the mountains do not flow consistently in either speed or direction. At one point, several hundred yards from shore, the twenty-four foot sailboat I helmed was hit by sudden gusts that spun the boat, in less than a minute, in a full three hundred sixty degree circle.

Sometimes we are blindsided. We try to predict with accuracy, and we move through our days with a sense of confidence, yet experience shows that sometimes life is as predictable as the winds on Lake Pend Oreille, or the weather in Seattle. What do you do when you get hit hard by The Unexpected? Your response at that point is critical to your success and sometimes to your survival. People panic, people freeze, people jump to frenetic action without forethought. But if you learn and practice Aviate, Navigate, Communicate—handling The Unexpected becomes a lesson from your experience that helps the rest of us as we too walk through life.

I teach a workshop called StoryTelling 101. The most basic element of a story is its conflict, an incident from your life where you faced a struggle, obstacle, hurdle, fight, disaster, pain, difficulty, problem or challenge. Everyone has them. No one plans what they will be; they are unexpected.

It's how you face the challenge, what steps you take, who helps you, what advice you receive, how you grow, what you learn and what you can pass on ... this is what makes a story. The Unexpected always represents some kind of challenge or conflict, and the story you take away from it has great value for all of us.

When Norman Dyhrenfurth put together plans for the first Americans to summit Mount Everest, one consideration was the need for oxygen when climbing at high altitude. Tom Hornbein, a medical doctor and member of the expedition, was put in charge of planning the oxygen equipment and the amount of oxygen needed for the climbers. This would be one of the basics for success in their adventure. Planning in advance for their oxygen needs was certainly wise, and planning ahead is something we teach our children to do.

But the story, as it relates to oxygen, really happens at the moment on the mountain when the team realized there wasn't enough oxygen. This is where the conflict occurs. Seattle native Jim Whittaker and Sherpa Nawang Gombu reached the summit of Everest on May 1, 1963 but at the summit, in the rarified atmosphere of 29,028 feet where the available oxygen is about a third of what it is at sea level, Whittaker's oxygen tank was empty. He and Gombu descended, but with impaired mental and physical capabilities. The second summit attempt was aborted only eight hundred feet below the summit because of limited oxygen.

Blaming—the first tactic we rally to our defense—went on for several days. Hornbein was blamed for inadequate planning; the two hundred sixteen bottles weren't enough. Climbers were blamed for using oxygen unnecessarily, breathing from the tanks at altitude while just sitting around doing nothing in particular.

Ultimately it's a story of facing and overcoming an obstacle and moving past it toward success, Eventually, at the end of the story, the expedition put six climbers on top of the world.

There were other obstacles and setbacks of course, including the death of John Breitenbach in the Khumbu Icefall. The Unexpected will happen. And it's The Unexpected, the conflict, the challenge that turns any event into a story. It's facing the barrier of running the four-minute mile, the barrier of flying faster than the speed of sound, the barrier of rock, snow, ice and altitude. And, more importantly, it's how you face the problem, how you find a solution and overcome it that turns something unpredicted in your life into a message of value for the rest of us. Knowing that's true gives meaning to The Unexpected and purpose when you're in the middle of it.

Overcoming variables is what makes it possible for you to continue on toward your vision. It's finding the wooden broom handle in the corner of the hangar, it's discovering expenditures that can be reduced, it's selling items from your garage for extra cash to pay an unexpected bill, it's finding a new place to land so you can fly again the next day on your journey. You start with the idea that you will probably get to your destination. You predict what will happen to the best of your ability. And you adjust and adapt to the chance variables that turn your journey into a real story.

THINK PAST THE END OF YOUR NOSE

When my kids were growing up I taught them: "Think past the end of your nose." I wanted them to learn to look down the road a ways, to be able to visualize, to set goals, to make plans. I also wanted them to think through the consequences of what they were doing at the moment. In essence, I was teaching them to make predictions about outcomes and to prepare for unexpected variations in their plans.

To "think past the end of your nose" means to exercise your ability to go beyond your present circumstances by thinking ahead, by thinking down the road. It's building on Aviate—getting control of the basics first of all. It's continuing with Navigate—seeing the present, visualizing the future, and route finding from here to there. It's confirming with Communicate—getting feedback along the way.

FEAR FACTOR

Ancient Scripture says, "Man makes his plans, and God directs his steps." It may be that divine intervention, causing unforeseeable events, interrupts your plans. Be very careful of letting the fear of unexpected events or circumstances, which is really a fear of the unknown, keep you from making plans. There is, after all, no chance of your steps being directed without making plans in the first place and without setting those plans in motion by stepping out the door and starting your journey. Sometimes we won't start something because, we say, we don't know how it will turn out. Really? Or is it because of fear? Maybe we're afraid that it won't turn out *in our favor*.

You can count on one thing—if you don't start, you'll never finish. Another scripture says, in so many words, "The lazy person says, 'There's a lion in the streets ... I could die out there!'" In other words, you can always find a reason not to take the first step out the door. You can always rationalize your way out of an attempt to try something, to do something you haven't done before, to tackle something in a new way. Fear of snakes is, to my thinking, normal. Fear of heights is healthy. Fear of failure is not. Finding excuses is nothing but fear of failure, and fear of failure is nothing but a guarantee that you won't take on a challenge, and not taking on the challenge guarantees that the world will be no better because of you. You are not here simply to occupy a chair, to take up space. You are here for a reason, and I'm going to guess that whatever that reason is, it does involve opening the door and stepping out. Perhaps it's a relationship, maybe it's a business venture, it could be wilderness exploration or getting up in front of a Toastmasters club to give a speech—but when your heart gets the call, when you see the vision, when the imagination of what's possible kicks into high gear, you must stand up, you must raise your hand and say "Me! I'll do it!"—you must go to the door, open it and step outside. Probably the lion is made of paper.

What are your plans? What do you predict will be the outcome if you get to where you want to go? With good planning, and with good execution of your plans, you'll probably get there. Be ready for the variables that will come. Expect The Unexpected. Think past the end of your nose. The rest of us will want to hear your stories because what we learn from you will help us in our own. You can count on that!

FUMES *and a* PRAYER

Logbook

FUMES *and a* PRAYER

CHAPTER SEVEN

EXPERIENCE

ex-pi-re-ence *noun* \ik-'spir-ē-ən(t)s\

doing something over and over so you get
good at it

FUMES *and a* PRAYER

EXPERIENCE

He was twenty-one years old. Flying a P-51D Mustang, Chuck Yeager was shot down by German Nazis over occupied France. He survived the parachute descent, landing in a pine forest. He had shrapnel punctures in his feet and hands, a hole in his right calf and a gash on his forehead. Shot down on March 5, 1944, he was taken in by the Maquis, the French resistance fighters, and on March 30 escaped to Spain, returning to England on May 15, 1944. It was just ten weeks after being shot down.

Chuck Yeager is one of my heroes. I have a great deal of admiration for those in the arena of any endeavor—music, sports, business, politics, education, safaris—where they face and accept obstacles, hurdles and challenges that most would back away from, if they ever got into the ring in the first place. Along with a deep desire to be just like them, and a disappointment that I am not, I am moved by the struggle, the fight, the determination, the dedication and pure grit. If they succeed, I am motivated to keep trying. If they don't succeed, my heart and soul are still moved by the valiant effort.

This is often quoted, yet I am moved every time I read it:

It is not the critic who counts, nor the man who points out how the strong man stumbled, or where the doer of the deeds could have done them better. The credit belongs to

139

the man who is actually in the arena; whose face is marred by dust and sweat and blood; who strives valiantly; who errs and comes short again and again; who knows the great enthusiasms, the great devotions; and spends himself in a worthy cause; who, at best, knows in the end the triumph of high achievement; and who, at worst, if he does fail, at least fails while daring greatly, so that his place shall never be with those cold and timid souls who know neither victory nor defeat.

—Theodore Roosevelt.

HABIT: TWENTY-ONE DAYS

The key element of experience is repetition. The adage, "practice makes perfect," with its corollary "practice makes permanent" is true. What most people don't realize is how much practice perfection and permanence takes! We accept the popular notion that we can develop a new habit in just twenty-one days.

A search on the internet for "develop a new habit in 21 days" reveals the concept to be so ubiquitous that you'd think one of the Biblical patriarchs came up with the idea long, long ago. Most of the articles say "research shows" or "there's a saying…" or "experts agree!" and the principle is just accepted as true. But very few seem to know where the idea came from.

But the 21-Day principle is not old. In 1960, a 61-yr old cosmetic surgeon named Maxwell Maltz wrote *Psycho-Cybernetics*. This is where the "21-Days to develop a new habit" idea seems to have begun. In his book, Maltz instructs readers to read chapter two three times each week for twenty-one days. From his observations, patients almost always took twenty-one days to adjust to a new face, or to lose the feeling of a "phantom" limb after amputation. He concludes that it takes the mind-body connection at least twenty-one days to adjust to any new mindset, shift in self image, or habit to become a viable part of one's life. The idea has spread so widely that most people accept it as common knowledge.

Aristotle said: "We are what we repeatedly do. Excellence then, is not an act, but a habit." Maltz might add: "as long as you do it at least twenty-one days in a row."

HABIT: SIXTY-SIX DAYS

Researchers at the University College London found something different. In their studies of "habit," where behavior becomes automatic, they discovered a range of time in forming a habit, especially in the areas of eating and exercise. They found no magic number of days. They saw people form habits in as few as eighteen days on the short end and up to two hundred fifty-four days on the long end. Some people take quite a while to get used to doing something new and doing it without thinking about it.

Search online for "forming habits" and discover not only many sites that use the now standard 21-day "rule" but also some who cite a 66-day standard. This comes from the University College London's study where the *average* time for an activity, or way of thinking, to become automatic was sixty-six days, and this is touted as how long it should take you too.

HABIT: TIME AND REPETITION

But when you see the range of eighteen to two hundred fifty-four days it took the people in their research, the idea of twenty-one days or sixty-six days becomes absurd. It will apparently take you however long it takes you, simple as that. How long it will actually take you to develop a new habit depends on several factors including how entrenched certain undesirable habits already have become and how strong your reason is for making a change.

I'm not trying to duplicate all the research and theories about motivation and habit. I hope you will not fall for any particular number of days as standard. Adjusting to a new hairstyle might take only three weeks, becoming familiar with the peculiarities of a new car might take longer, and accepting that you now eat only half as much as you used to could take quite a while!

More importantly, I hope you will see that what you want to become automatic will take time and repetition. So you practice your scales for hours upon hours in order to become proficient at the keyboard. And you practice emergency procedures frequently during training flights so when you need them in real life, you perform automatically. The point of having a habit is that when you need it, it's there for you without having to think about it.

EXPERIENCE

In his autobiography, General Chuck Yeager describes what it took to become the first man in history to break the sound barrier. Surviving required every scrap of experience he'd accumulated over the years … to the point where even an hour less experience might have made a difference in some the circumstances where he found himself. His instincts were supplemented by the knowledge he gained from conducting hundreds of spin tests, and his experience kept him from being as disoriented as he otherwise would have been. He flew more than anybody else, and that, he says, is what made him good.

The point of experience is habit.

The point of habit is survival when The Unexpected happens.

Of course, habits can be good or bad. Either way, they're developed by repeated experience. If a habit is bad, it's bad because it gets in the way of something you want to have or achieve. If a habit is good, it's good for the opposite reason. A good habit is your friend because it helps you get something, go somewhere, become something.

Let's say you want to change the habit of arriving late wherever you go. It's a bad habit because your goal is to win friends, influence people and make a living which requires you to meet people on an appointment basis. Your experience has been negative because being late is frowned upon by your prospects and by your friends. To change that habit requires the repeated experience of at least arriving on time, at best arriving early.

When I taught classes to real estate agents who wanted to have a successful visit at the home a of prospective seller, what we call a "listing presentation," I told them to arrive in front of the house ten to fifteen minutes early without fail, but wait to go to the front door. They were to use the extra time to drive the neighborhood and get a feel for the area, to see how well people cared for their homes and to notice how the seller's home was situated in the neighborhood. At exactly the time of the appointment, the agent rang the doorbell or knocked on the door.

It's amazing how many people notice when you are punctual. For many of you, being punctual may be an important new habit. Arriving on time or early as a habit requires one thing: arriving on time or early consistently over a period of time, until doing so becomes automatic. You don't even think about it any more.

Brushing your teeth, exercising, eating right, going to bed on time, setting aside time to journal, answering sales objections effectively, reading to your kids, saving, driving safely (not tailgating, not speeding, not cursing the other driver) … every activity you want to become automatic requires just one thing: doing it consistently over time.

STARTING POINT

If you work on the basics of your venture or enterprise before something unexpected happens, how much easier will it be to respond automatically if you've already focused on the basics and practice them every day? Let's say you and your spouse decide to get a handle on your family finances. You have not been saving and you decide to develop the habit. You begin putting ten percent of your paycheck into a savings account every payday. Life is good. As time goes on and your account grows you become less fearful about anything unexpected. When the day comes that your transmission goes out (my experience is that this is more of a process than an instant event but still, there will come a day…) then you will be ready for it. The day the transmission stops transmitting is a little late to start saving for it. But if you focused on this basic element of family life, your finances, when the transmission unexpectedly goes out, you're ready for it.

EXPERIENCE

Years ago I read a book on professional driving. I was not and am not a professional driver, but it was an interesting read. One tip I found was always to have an out, always to know where other vehicles are positioned around you and to know where you could suddenly and safely swerve in case of emergency in front of you. I started to practice that every time I was on the freeway. I noticed the other day that I was still doing that. Driving Interstate 5 from Tacoma to Seattle during early rush hour traffic with constant rain, I knew where the other cars were beside, in front and behind me. I knew I could pull over immediately to the left shoulder (the other main reason to drive the carpool lane) and if the car in front of me suddenly did the same thing, I would then have that empty spot in front of me.

Chuck Yeager didn't start out experienced and neither do you. He had his first hour of flight one day, then his second, then his third and so on. The brilliant thing Yeager did was to volunteer to fly every time an opportunity came up. On purpose he flew often, until he had accumulated thousands of hours of piloting time.

INSTANT GRATIFICATION

Any habit starts with the first step. You must start there. The tricky thing is that the first step is often the hardest of them all. I believe this is because you wish you were now where you want to be down the road, after you've acquired the habit. You want to get fit— you visualize what you'll look like and what you'll be able to do and how you'll feel. It will be good. The problem is you want it now. Call it a by-product of an instant gratification society. But habits don't work that way. A habit starts with the first step on the track or trail. It continues with the second step, and so on until that day's workout is complete. The next day requires the same. So does the third day, and the fourth day, and on and on.

You cannot look at the start of a new habit as anything more than a day at a time. You start with the end in mind, design the steps to get there, and in a sense forget about the end and focus on the step in front of you. If you've done a good job of picturing where you want to go and how you're going to get there, then you don't need to keep concentrating on the result. Take the steps and you'll get there. Focus on the steps. Take the first one. The next one will be easier. One day, driving on the freeway, you'll discover you've developed a habit and you don't even have to think about it anymore—it's automatic!

EXCELLENCE AND PERFECTION

I worked at The Boeing Aircraft Company twice. The first time was a two-year stint as a flight test mechanic working on the very first Boeing 767. It was a few years later when I worked on the military production line building tankers from 707s.

One of my friends who worked with me was a perfectionist. When building an airplane from aluminum sheets and rivets, it's important that rivets be installed correctly. Angles, braces and sheets of aluminum overlap and to connect them where they overlap holes are drilled for rivets to be used. The appropriate size rivet is pressed into the hole, a pneumatic rivet gun pounds on the head side while a bucking bar causes the rivet tail to flatten and widen, thus securely holding the parts together. Engineers determine acceptable tolerances of height and width of the rivet tail.

EXPERIENCE

The rivet gun doesn't shoot anything ... it's more like a small, handheld jackhammer, though it sounds kind of like a machine gun and it's a good idea to wear ear plugs when operating one. But it can bounce. If the operator isn't careful the die, the part of the rivet gun that pounds on the rivet head, can jump a bit and put a smiley face on the rivet head.

Again, engineering has acceptable limits on how much damage to the rivet head is acceptable. A little smiley face won't matter. You can see it, but it does not affect the structural strength of the installed rivet.

My friend, the perfectionist, could not stand to see a smiley face on any rivet he installed on the aircraft, and he installed a lot of them. If any smiley face appeared on a rivet he'd just installed, he drilled it out and replaced it with another one. He did that a lot, which meant he was sometimes behind on his production schedule.

One day at lunch I figured it out. I said, "John, you're trying to make the airplane a work of art. It isn't a work of art. It's a machine. Not every rivet has to be installed like a Rembrandt. If it's within acceptable limits, you have to let it go for the sake of getting airplanes out the door on time."

John could rivet parts together very well. He'd installed thousands of them. His way of doing it had become a habit, but he carried it too far. There is a difference between perfection and excellence, and you need to know which you really need so that you don't waste time and energy pursuing perfection if you don't need to.

Make no mistake—I am a huge believer in excellence. I used to be called a perfectionist (until I'd messed up so many things that people stopped thinking of me that way) and one day it occurred to me that nothing on the planet is technically perfect (though it would be a good idea, men, to say to your wife that she is perfect!). It was pointless to pursue perfection. But it would be very useful and rewarding to pursue excellence.

Excellence is a fuzzy term in general. To you, in a specific circumstance or a particular venture, the standard of excellence might be higher, lower or even different than for someone else. For John, excellence meant no smiley faces on rivets he installed in the airplane. For others around him, excellence meant no smiley faces beyond what the engineering standards allowed.

PERSONAL EXCELLENCE

There was a small business next to a taxiway at Boeing Field in south Seattle. The company ran a delivery service using small airplanes. They picked up packages anywhere in the Northwest where there was at least a small airstrip and flew them anywhere else in the Northwest where there was at least a small airstrip. The company pilots flew mostly at night. Working in the shop was someone with years of experience and the highest mechanic license, an AI—Airworthiness Inspector. Another mechanic was also licensed and did all the same work the boss mechanic did, but could not sign off airplane logbooks for certain inspections that required the advanced license.

If you are the aircraft mechanic working there, you take a walk one morning out to the airplane parking area where the company airplanes were tied down. As you walk past one of the airplanes, you notice the side passenger door slightly ajar. You try to latch it closed, but it won't close. You look closely at the door. It appears to be slightly crooked, and upon closer examination you see one of the two hinges is broken. You know this is new damage but the dent on the side of the airplane that matches the edge of the door when it's fully opened clues you to the likely explanation. The pilot flying this plane the night before probably had not completely latched the door. When he took, off the door came open, and the force of the air stream slammed the door back against the side of the airplane and broke the hinge.

Of course, the pilot reported neither the incident nor the damage … probably hadn't even seen the damage. But you see it, and you show it to your boss, the experienced mechanic. You know for sure the airplane cannot be flown with the door in that condition, that a new hinge will be ordered and you will install it. You tow the plane into the shop.

The boss mechanic says he will take care of it. The company wants to have the airplane available that night, and the repair will have to be done quickly. You go off to work on another airplane.

Toward quitting time you wander over to the damaged airplane to see how the repair is coming. But what you see is not what you expected. There is no new hinge on the door, although the door is now shut and latched. Leaning closer for a good look, you see that the boss mechanic repaired the broken hinge, but not with a new one, and not with a used one. He used wire. He used wire in exactly the same sense as when we say something is held together with baling wire, meaning it's been jerry-rigged. It is sloppy. It is holding the door shut, but you know the FAA would not approve because it is not a safe repair.

You find the boss, the experienced mechanic, and you ask him why he has repaired the hinge with wire. He explains that the company needs to fly the plane tonight, that a new part has been ordered but will take a day or two to get, and that this will be OK as long as nobody sees it.

You scratch your head. What? You know this isn't right and certainly not safe. If that wire doesn't hold and the door slams open again in flight at 170 miles an hour or so, the door could rip off, hit the tail, possibly damage the elevator and at worst bring the airplane, its cargo and its pilot down. You would never have installed such a repair on an airplane. It should be grounded until a proper repair is completed. You know this is not even in the same ballpark as excellence; it is, in fact, shoddy.

The experienced mechanic tells you that it will be OK, suggests you not tell anyone, reminds you that he'll put the correct part on as soon as it arrives, and releases the airplane for flight that night. One more thing he tells you … if you report this to the company, he will see to it that you don't work there any more.

Fortunately for the pilot that night, nothing bad happened. But you must make a tough decision. Your decision is based on what level of excellence you are willing to embrace. Will you accept his baling wire level of excellence (though you can't bring yourself to call it excellence) or is your standard of excellence based on safety, on accepted FAA standards and on ethics? You decide you cannot work there any more. You cannot work for a boss who covers up shoddy work, who risks the safety of the plane and pilot and who demands your secrecy about it—all under threat of your employment. You resign that day.

This is a true story, and I was that mechanic. I understood that using wire to hold down a broken latch on a car would pose no danger. I also understood that an emergency landing somewhere in the jungles of Wagga-Wagga Land where head hunters abound, where mosquitoes nearly match the size of your airplane and where plenty of big snakes would like to squeeze you into a lunch-size package … right there, my standard of excellence might be lowered.

Better to risk a door flopping open than to spend the afternoon in a boiling pot or in the belly of a python!

Excellence is variable. Excellence is a level, a standard where you are pleased with your work, where under your circumstances and the criteria and resources you've been given, you have passed mere acceptability and reached toward perfection.

I presume the experienced mechanic I worked for considered his work excellent. It was certainly creative, and he did meet his boss's desire to have the plane flying that night. For me, excellence meant the plane was airworthy—the repair had to meet FAA standards and be safe to fly, and the company needed to get the part that day or find another way to pick up that airplane's payload that night.

In any venture, you must decide what the level of excellence is for you. My mother sewed her own clothes, but she did not allow any of us to see her work until it was finished. If a hem or a seam was crooked, she ripped it out, sewed it again until it was excellent. Then, and only then, we could see her work, and it was always beautiful. If Mom had lived during the Oregon Trail days and needed to sew for sixteen kids and have them ready before the trek westward which was in two weeks, you know the standard of excellence would have been different than when she sat in her comfortable sewing room with plenty of time to do her work.

THE 10,000-HOUR RULE

Experience and excellence go hand in hand. Like a mathematical equation, adding experience equals more excellence. Even negative experience can take you on the path to excellence as long as you learn from it. My experience over northern Colorado was negative, but from it I learned to apply Aviate, Navigate, Communicate to the rest of my life. As long as the intent is to improve, experience leads to excellence.

In the book *Outliers*, Malcolm Gladwell explains the "10,000-Hour Rule." Based on a study by Anders Ericsson, currently a Professor of Psychology at Florida State University, Gladwell points out that becoming excellent in any venture—chess, violin, hockey, cooking, public speaking, computer savvy—takes about 10,000 hours of practice and experience to reach world-class status. If you practice a particular task for twenty hours every week, you will achieve greatness in about ten years. Do it full time, forty hours each week, and get there in just five years.

Before the Beatles became world famous, they were a struggling high school band. In August, 1960, the "Silver Beatles," as they had been called up to this time, traveled to Hamburg, Germany where, at a club called Indra, they changed their name to just "The Beatles." Shortly after, the Indra shut down and the Beatles moved to another, bigger club, the Kaiserkeller Club, and performed eight hours a day, seven days a week, from 1960 to 1964. During that time they amassed more than 10,000 hours live playing time, thus shaping their talent and style, sounding like no one else when they returned to Liverpool.

John Lennon revealed in an interview, "We got better and got more confidence. We couldn't help it, with all the experience, playing all night long.... We had to try even harder, put our heart and soul into it, to get ourselves over." And the rest is history.

In Ericsson's study during the 1990s, he and his team studied student musicians at the Berlin Academy of Music. The musicians, all talented but none "gifted," were divided into three groups based on excellence. The highest group was the elite, the middle group was the good, the lowest group was the average. Ericsson and his team discovered one quantifiable difference between the groups. All had begun their music training around age five, but the difference was in the intervening years—the amount of solitary practice time. The average group of musicians had accumulated around 2,000 hours of practice time by the time they turned twenty. That sounds like a lot of time. But the really good players, in the same timeframe, had accumulated about 5,000 hours. More amazing still, the elite musicians had accumulated around 10,000 hours of practice. And that's how you get to be a world-class musician!

Ericsson explains that the principle applies to other types of experts as well, such as chess players and athletes. If you want to be world-class, to be among the elite in your area of interest, plan right now how you will accumulate your 10,000 hours of solitary, concerted, deliberate practice. In other words, you need experience.

Of course, most of us are not world class and will not become world class, nor do we need to be world class to become everything we want to be and to make a difference in people's lives while we walk on this planet—we all want that dash on the tombstone to matter in some way. I believe you do want to make a difference through your activity or venture or business, and to do so you will have to get experience. You will need to practice, to perform, and to process the feedback you get along the way. You will need to know the basics of your activity (Aviate); you will need to know where you are, where you want to go, and how you'll get there (Navigate); you'll need to have feedback along the way (Communicate) so you'll know how you're doing and if you need any course corrections.

Experience Is Not Just Putting in Time

There are exceptions to the 10,000-Hour Rule, and it's very possible for you to be one of them. Not every venture requires being world class, not every competition requires being among the elite. When Chuck Yeager took the controls of the Bell X-1 on October 14, 1947—the day he became the first man in history to fly at supersonic speed, the day he proved to naysayers that there was no "demon" at the sound barrier, the day he drew on all his training and experience and skill as a fighter pilot and as a test pilot—on that day as Chuck Yeager entered the cockpit of the Bell X-1 and took its controls, he had accumulated in his logbook a total of just 1,452 hours of flight time. Not 10,000, not 5,000 and not even 2,000 hours. He may not have had as many flight hours as other test pilots either military or civilian. In Yeager's case, it was not just the number of hours of experience that made him qualified to fly the Bell X-1. It wasn't just the number of hours that made him skillful as a pilot.

It was for Yeager, as it will be for you, what you *do* with those hours, however many they may be, that will set the stage for success. What you do with the hours, combined with Opportunity as you will see in chapter nine, will make all the difference.

When Yeager took an assignment at Wright Field near the end of World War II, he found the air base crammed full of all kinds of fighter planes. Wright Field was the site for the first conversions of propeller-driven airplanes to jet and rocket propulsion. Two weeks after arriving at Wright, Yeager flew the first operational American jet fighter, the Lockheed P-80 Shooting Star. Yeager was in a flight test division of fighter planes. His job as an assistant maintenance officer was to fly any airplane that had been worked on or had received an engine conversion to make sure the plane worked well.

EXPERIENCE

He could fly as much as he wanted in a wide variety of aircraft, and he took advantage of it. As a maintenance officer, he was not among the twenty-five or so test pilots, and without a college degree he doubted he could be one of them.

With a competitor's spirit, Yeager often climbed into a P-51, took it to altitude and waited for a test pilot to take off, then dove at them, challenging them to a dogfight. The test pilots had no combat experience, while dogfighting was Yeager's love and his combat background. Yeager was unmatched.

The key to Yeager's success, and what set him apart from the others, was what he did with his hours in the air—and there were plenty of hours. He flew six to eight hours a day, and during each flight he tried to learn something new—what an unfamiliar switch was for, how the airplane operated in unusual weather, and the various systems on the aircraft. In other words, he practiced, and he practiced on purpose. He practiced to get better. He practiced to be the best.

How about you? When you do your work or your music or your business or whatever your venture is, do you do it on purpose? Is everyday a practice day in which you look for ways to improve, ways to learn, ways to adapt? How will you ever get better if you do the same things in the same ways day after day after day?

Experience *is* about putting in the hours, by definition … but not that alone. Experience is what you get *out* of those hours—hours in which you practice on purpose.

My friend David is six feet, five inches, tall. He attended the University of Washington where he learned the maxim, "Six feet, two, you're on the crew," the crew being the University's rowing team. Crewing is done in an eight-man shell—a long, narrow and streamlined boat, easy for the uninitiated to tip over but speedy in the hands and oars of a skilled crew. I've watched David row his single-seat scull on nearby American Lake. He makes it look easy. I've tried it myself. It isn't easy, as I found out when a little wobble caused a loss of balance and I fell out of the boat and into the lake—at which time I realized David had shown me how to get into the boat from the dock, but not how to get *back* into the boat from a floating position next to the boat in a hundred feet of water.

David loves to row. It is his love and his passion. When he started rowing on American Lake, he practiced every day. He left early, before dark; he rowed his course and was back at the dock before the sun came up. Coached by his older brother, an Olympic contender in kayaking, he pushed himself every day in several kinds of exercises. On one day he rowed from buoy to buoy, full out from one to the next, moderately between the next two, full out between the next two in a pattern that runners also use to keep the heart rate up at a workout level throughout the exercise. Another day he would row with all his might for one minute, row moderately for another minute, then row like a sprinter for two minutes, moderately for two, and then row full speed, as hard as he could for three full minutes, then rest and repeat. He especially worked on the most important part of a race, the start—those first several seconds where you can pull out ahead, set the pace and gain the psychological advantage of being in the lead.

David logged every single day of practice on a chart. Whatever type of workout he did, he wrote it down. He recorded the times, the weather, the water conditions and how he felt every day. He rowed every day, and he rowed on purpose.

After just several months of hard training, David entered a race. Competitive by nature, and lean, with the long, powerful muscles of an endurance athlete, David and his wife traveled from Tacoma, Washington, to Sand Point, Idaho, on Lake Pend Oreille, the same lake I sailed on in those swirly winds. Competitors came from all over the Northwest: Washington, Oregon, Idaho and Montana. Lined up on the shore, the colorful array of rowing shells looked like missiles sliced in half length-wise, waiting to shoot across the lake, propelled by arms and legs, hearts and lungs of scullers seeking speed, sport and open space.

Among other competitors walking the beach, a big man swaggered, his muscled arms and legs evidence of hard work at the gym. He was experienced and was the favorite to win this race. David's wife pointed the man out and said to David, "That's your competition."

The starting gun signaled the racers to pull their first stroke, and David rowed with all his might, just as he had in training, to get the advantage right at the start. After just five quick starting strokes—half, half, three-quarter, three-quarter, full—followed by ten strokes at full power, David had the lead and settled into the repetitive oar in, stroke, oar up, return, oar in, stroke, oar up, return... With every stroke, in every minute, over every mile, David drew from the lessons learned during those early morning hours of practice.

The race lasted less than an hour, "thankfully," said David, "as the course had been shortened due to extremely rough water conditions—waves churned into frothing, white-capped foam, blown by a stiff, bone-chilling wind, especially for summer." For this too David had prepared during those practice days in the dark, when rain blown horizontal still found his blinking, red bow-light plying the rough waters back home. When the race was over, David took home the first-place trophy, beating even the crowd favorite. David hadn't practiced 10,000 hours, but he hadn't needed to. What he did do was practice on purpose. He practiced daily; he practiced to improve, and he worked hard at it.

Two years later, David entered the biggest open-water race in the northwest United States, The Great Cross Sound race, starting at Alki Beach in Seattle, rowing four miles across Puget Sound to Blakely Rock off Bainbridge Island, then over a mile to Decatur Reef at the southeast corner of the island, and returning to Alki Point, a total of about seven and a half miles. The race included ninety-six boats with competitors from all over the western U.S. and Canada. The Great Cross Sound includes both single and two-man shells, and kayaks as well. Starting off at 9:30 AM, David fought strong winds, huge ferries and his own fatigue, and he finished fifty-eight minutes, fifty-six seconds later, a time that again gave him the first place trophy, beating all boats in all categories.

Would 10,000 hours of practice have earned him a higher place? No. There were no bigger trophies to take home that day—David had the biggest one. He led the field, he finished first overall, and he took home the champion's trophy. What he did do was practice—and practice on purpose—to be the best in his field in the competition he chose. Was his aim to be a world champion? Was his goal to stand on the highest box as an Olympic champion with an auditorium filled with thousands of admiring spectators and fans while listening to the national anthem? No. Was his goal to have his face on a Wheaties box? No. Was he hoping for Nike or other sports companies to endorse him for millions of dollars? No.

David wanted to be the best in the Northwest. And he achieved that. His goals fit his life—he was married, had three kids, had a career, worked with troubled kids in the community, taught a Sunday School class … and he rowed.

EXPERIENCE

Experience has no substitute. If you want to be among the world's elite, log your 10,000 hours. If you want to lead the field in your neck of the woods, log whatever hours you will need in order to be in front. If you want to be really good at what you do, get experience. Practice, and practice on purpose.

TRADEOFFS

Very few of us are among the elite in anything. If you are, the principles in this book will help you, especially when The Unexpected shows up one day. For the rest of us, the thing we choose to get really good at has to balance out with the other aspects of our lives. There comes a point where you reach a limit, a tradeoff point. Everything you pursue has a tradeoff, and you have to decide where that tradeoff is. If you row a narrow, missile-shaped shell, or climb a glacier-draped mountain, or start a business in real estate, or get married ... to pursue your venture requires a tradeoff.

As you gain experience in your venture, as you put in the hours and hours of practice and performance, remember that there is a cost. If you will be either world-class or best-in-class at anything, you will be forced to choose between time spent pursuing your venture and time spent pursuing the rest of life.

In business this is called "opportunity cost." To invest dollars in new tooling, for instance, means you will not have the opportunity to spend those same dollars in marketing, or in recruiting, or in more floor space. The opportunity you *don't* take because you *do* take another one is the "opportunity cost."

The same applies to all of life. To invest time in practicing your golf swing at the driving range is to take away the opportunity to invest that time with your kids. Though I am not anywhere near saying that investing time in any single thing is right or wrong for you, I am saying that you must count the cost, the cost of opportunities lost, the tradeoff for pursuing your goals. You must decide what it is you are willing to trade to get the experience you need in your venture—just be aware that for everything, there is a tradeoff. As the old Crusader tells Indiana Jones regarding which goblet to drink from, "Choose wisely."

GOOD, BAD, UGLY

One problem of practicing just because you have to, like a child taking piano or violin lessons, or ballet or gymnastics or figure skating, is that when mistakes are made they are not corrected. Instead, the good and the bad are all practiced together, repeated again and again until both become habit. My golf game does not improve for just one reason—without knowing what to improve, I just keep doing the same swing over and over and over. My elbows aren't right, my stance isn't correct, my head and shoulder position isn't effective simply because I do not know what they should be, so I don't work on improving them, and therefore I don't get better. Practice simply for the sake of practice builds habits, and those habits include everything I do that's right and everything I do that's wrong.

EXPERIENCE

Experience that leads to better and better habits has to be done on purpose. You have to get the experience with the purpose of doing it better, of improving the performance, of reducing errors.

The Aviate-Navigate-Communicate of Golf

A weekend golfer at best, I learned to golf from Bob, a friend who, on my first time at the local nine-hole golf course, kept answering my pleas for advice with, "Just hit the ball." I love to compete, and my golfing mission in life has been to beat Bob. I have never beaten Bob—which is perhaps the natural conclusion to following his advice. I never got better because I kept doing the same things over and over.

Until, that is, the day I picked up a book for weekend golfers by Jack Nicklaus. He wrote the book for those golfers like me who go to the course for the fun of it. I enjoy the outdoors, the grass and the trees. Especially the trees. I seem to spend a lot of golf time among the trees! I'm quite sure that most golf balls are designed to fly straight down the fairway while a select few are designed to slice or hook whenever and wherever there are trees. Those are the golf balls I buy, apparently.

I learned the most basic element of golf from Bob: Hit the ball. Aviate.

I knew where I was (the tee) and where I wanted to go (the green) and how I wanted to get there (straight down the fairway). Navigate.

Now, with Jack Nicklaus's book in the bag, I had my coach, someone who knew what I wanted to do and told me how to do it. Communicate.

I got one thing from Nicklaus's book. There was more, of course, but over the years just one thing has stuck in my memory, a lesson to take with me on every visit to the golf course. Not only that, it's a lesson I now take into every area where I endeavor to improve—writing, public speaking, sailing, flying, and even marriage. This one thing sped up my progress in becoming a better public speaker, and I coach public speakers first and foremost to practice this one thing. It's not a surprising tactic, once you think about it, but very few people do it.

The lesson was this: Don't try to improve your grip, your stance, your elbows, your upswing, your downswing, your follow through, your head position ... don't try to improve any two or more at the same time. Whenever you go to the golf course to work on your game, work on one thing and one thing only. Next time you visit the course, you can work on another thing if you want to, but again it can only be one thing. One thing at a time.

IF I WERE YOUR COACH

People who want to become better speakers need to get up and speak. They need to learn how to bring interesting and appropriate content, how to organize and structure a speech, how to include humor and where to include it, how to engage an audience in the first words they say, how to articulate their words and project their voice, how to use their hands, how to manage the stage or whatever area they have available to move in, and more.

The typical agenda most speakers have when they get up to speak is to work on several of these at the same time. I say, don't do that.

EXPERIENCE

If I were your coach and you wanted to become a better speaker, then every time you speak I would tell you to just work on one thing. You will get better at that one thing in a shorter time, and thereby get better at all things in a shorter time, if you focus on just one element of speaking every time you get up in front of an audience.

As a member of Toastmasters for several years, I have given a number of practice speeches. Toastmasters is a comfortable place to learn. You receive positive feedback along with encouragement in areas where you can improve. One day I prepared a speech for one of the clubs where I was a member, and like the proverbial lightbulb coming on, my brain connected the dots between learning to be a better weekend golfer and learning to be a better public speaker. Aha! I saw it.

Before the club meeting started, I explained to Cosette, my evaluator that day, that while she would fill in her comments for my particular speech in the Toastmasters speech manual, I wanted her to watch for one thing. For this speech, I wasn't going to care what else I could be working on; I knew I needed to work on better eye contact with audience members. I tend to see a group, no matter how large or how small, as an individual, and I tend to scan the audience quickly which gives me the feeling that I'm engaging them. But I could do better. I asked Cosette to watch for eye contact. My goal was to spend two seconds at a time of eye-to-eye contact with each audience member, and especially I wanted to look at one person and engage their attention for the first complete sentence of my opening.

Forgetting about every element of public speaking except for purposeful eye contact, I gave my seven-minute speech. I don't remember what I said; I don't remember the topic. I do remember to this day the faces of those in the audience because that day I saw them as individuals, not as a group. That was huge for me. I have never had to work on that again. The power of focusing on that one thing, eye contact, for seven minutes, drove the habit deep into my public speaking psyche, so that today I look at individuals in an audience eye-to-eye.

If I were your coach, and if I knew where you were and where you want to go and how you plan to get there, and if you wanted to get better at it, I would tell you as Jack Nicklaus told me, "practice one element of your endeavor at a time—not more."

You must try this!

THE ROAD TO SUCCESS

There's an old saying: "The road to success is paved with failure." Really? If that's true, then I'd be a great, world-class success by now, because I've failed a lot. Think about it. Is it really failure that leads to success? No. It's what you learn from your experiences, both from failure and from success. It's not the failure itself, it's what you experience—more specifically, it's what you learn from your experience. It's not as catchy, but the saying should go something like, "The road to success is paved with *lessons learned from* failure."

In the end, win or lose, triumph or tragedy, succeed or fail, use it all for experience, learn from that experience and develop habits that will last a lifetime. Continual improvement takes time. It requires practicing on purpose, positive learning from both success and failure, And it takes staying power in the arena—if your venture is worthy, don't give up. Determine not to join "those cold and timid souls who know neither victory nor defeat." Learn, grow, succeed and achieve from your experience.

Practice on purpose!

FUMES *and a* PRAYER

Logbook

FUMES *and a* PRAYER

CHAPTER EIGHT

RISK

risk *noun* \'risk\

possibility of danger, injury or loss

FUMES *and a* PRAYER

RISK

It is impossible to escape risk. You cannot live life without risk. Even if you say that you avoid risk by not trying anything, you accept a risk—the risk of boredom, of illness, of an early death from lack of exercise, in which case you become the proverbial couch potato. It is the risk of rotting along with the consequences thereof.

On the other end of the spectrum, there are some people who take on a challenge with an attitude of reckless abandonment, seeming to ignore even the possibility of risk. These are the people of movies and television shows that glorify very dangerous stunts performed by actors who are stuntmen; or worse, those who attempt the same stunts with neither the training nor the experience of the stuntmen who star in the movies—and some might question the sanity of those stuntmen who would perform these stunts just to make a movie and get some laughs.

CALCULATED RISKS

In between the two extremes of couch potatoes and extremists is the world where most of us live. We take risks, but they are calculated risks, and we take measures to limit those risks from getting out of hand. So, the mountain climber takes climbing classes, starts with smaller peaks and simpler rock faces, buys the latest gear and clothing, follows guides, ropes up on slopes where an uncontrolled fall would be disastrous, and so on. Calculating the risk, the climber limits the chance of failure—meaning at best not making the summit and at worst suffering a fatal injury—by training hard, increasing skill, equipping sufficiently and gaining experience. Through knowledge of the mountains and their dangers, along with the necessary resources to navigate and survive, the climber is able to enjoy the exhilaration of living at the edge and still coming home for dinner.

Mount Rainier was first seen by Captain George Vancouver, a European explorer, in 1791. I saw the mountain as a fourteen-year-old boy when my dad, my family and I came back from Dad's three-year Air Force tour of duty near London, England, and we moved to our second house in Lynnwood, Washington.

Riding my bike on my paper route, with the newspaper bag over the front handles, I rode down a hill every day where Mount Rainier was visible seventy miles to the south. Our neighbor had climbed the mountain, and I could see through my bedroom window where he set his climbing boots to dry and to absorb the Sno-Seal waterproofing treatment he'd just applied. It was this neighbor who first got me interested in climbing a mountain before I ever asked him about it.

To a young teenaged boy, the lure was inescapable. I dreamed of the mountains, I read many books from the library—Annapurna, K2, Americans on Everest—and lived vicariously the experiences of those who had faced the snow, ice and rock, who had accepted the risks and who sometimes suffered but who, nevertheless, represented a challenge I could taste and a class of men to which I wanted to belong. I looked longingly at the mountain to the south.

RISK

In high school, my parents wisely told me that if I wanted to climb mountains I would have to take a course in mountaineering, and I was excited to do so. Three of us from Meadowdale High School attended the Seattle Mountaineers climbing course, going to an auditorium in Everett every week for lectures, slides and demonstrations, and traveling into the Cascades periodically for training in climbing rock cliffs, belaying a climbing partner, using the various hardware of climbing craft, descending into glacial crevasses to practice using prusik slings to ascend the climbing rope and thereby "rescue" ourselves ... glorious days to me. And still, every day, the mountain rose up two and three-quarters miles from nearly sea level, calling me to its glaciers, to its rock and, ultimately, to its quarter-mile wide summit crater.

This is why we accept risk. Something calls us. Whether it's a business venture, an outdoor adventure, a relationship, an activity—something inherent to the challenge beckons us, reaches into our heart and tugs, sometimes gently, sometimes fiercely, always tenaciously so that to ignore its call would leave us feeling vacant, a portion of our personhood missing, an unanswerable question persisting, "What if I had ...?" It's our nature to answer such calls, and not to do so leaves us lacking, unfulfilled and unable to contribute to the rest of the world what we would have offered if only we had taken on the challenge.

In the middle of my junior year in high school we moved to Lakewood, just south of Tacoma, Washington. The local mall, what was then the Villa Plaza, had many stores and shops and, most importantly to me, a mountain climbing and skiing equipment store. The Chalet was owned by Lou Whittaker, twin brother of Jim Whittaker, and the first time I visited the store, I looked out the window at the back and there was Mount Rainier, now only forty crow-flying miles away and looming twice the size of what it looked like from Lynnwood.

That mountain moved me, stirring my deepest sense of challenge and adventure, so that when I got word that the local mountaineering club in Tacoma was going on a summit climb on Rainier, I signed up. The route from the east side of the mountain takes two days to get to the summit, a third day to hike back off the mountain, and a fourth day to trek through the forests and back to the trailhead. On the first evening of the trek, we set up camp at Glacier Basin around timberline at 6,000 feet.

As a high school kid, on a high school kid's budget, my equipment was very basic. Instead of a nice, synthetic mountain tent with a rainfly, I had scrounged up a yellow, plastic tube tent which was literally a tube about eight feet long and two and a half feet in diameter. You closed off one end with snow or rocks and propped up the other end with a short pole, then threw in your sleeping bag with the foot toward the far, closed off end. Though basic, it worked.

What didn't work was freeze-dried food, rehydrated in a small cooking pot I'd brought, but with no stove to heat it in. This being my first "major" climb, it was a good thing I was with a group of experienced people. Sheepishly I shared my plight with two guys whose tent was pitched next to mine and with whom I'd become acquainted on the hike in, and they offered to let me use their little propane mountain stove. As I recall, those (mostly) rehydrated green peas and the stew were delicious! Sleeping through the night in the mountains has never come easy for me, and in this case was made more difficult thanks to a noisy nocturnal chipmunk exploring the edges of my tube tent and looking for rehydrated crumbs.

RISK

On day two we left the forest edge and ascended the lower slopes of Rainier alternating between snow and rock. The big challenge was the wind and snow. Wind was one thing ... when it whipped up the dry snow from the surface of the snow fields, it was another. While a light snow fell, the wind-driven crystals stuck to my woolen pants legs, melted just enough from body heat to wick moisture into the fibers of wool and then freeze, so that by the time we reached Camp Sherman at the head of Steamboat Prow at 9,500 feet, the lower twelve inches or so of my pants legs banged stiffly around my calves and shins.

The wind and blowing snow did not let up, and by morning, the snow had curled around the opening of my yellow tube tent and partially enveloped the head of my sleeping bag. Waiting as long as I could, I eventually crawled out of my tube tent to even worse weather. Word came from the group's leaders that the forecast was worsening, and eventually a decision was made to go back down and save the summit for another trip.

First Attempts

First attempts at anything are sometimes met with failure. The downside of risking anything is that you might not achieve your objective or, perhaps worse, you might suffer loss or injury. You may lose your reputation or your investment, a friendship or other relationship, your credit, cash or car. If it is an activity, you may lose toes to frostbite, suffer from Montezuma's revenge, a concussion, contusion or acute injury.

While those things could be suffered on your first try, your second try or your hundredth try, if you fail on your first attempt at anything, loss or injury of some sort and to some degree is likely. That's not the problem. The problem with failing on first attempts is that most people give up and don't try again. The old idea is a good one, I think: the best thing you can do when you fall off a horse is to get right back on it.

A TWO-EDGED SWORD

No matter what the venture and no matter its scope, I believe the central factor is a two-edged sword—the hope of success, and the possibility of failure. On one side there is a goal, a bounty to obtain. If you succeed, the prize is yours. This is the carrot in front of you, and the possibility of grasping that carrot motivates and drives us.

The other side, of course, is that venturing out, taking risks, means that you could fail. Out of every one hundred who have made it to the summit of Mount Everest, nine have died trying. Of those who desired to be on the first trans-Atlantic voyage of the Titanic, only 38% of the passengers and crew survived. The U.S. Small Business Association shows that only two-thirds of all small business startups survive the first two years and less than half make it to four years. And in marriage in the United States, around fifty percent of first-time marriages fail, sixty-six percent of second marriages fail, and nearly seventy-five percent of third marriages fail.

It's a good mindset to have: "Failure is not an option." Reality says that sometimes it happens to the best of us.

RISK

WHEN TO WORRY

In 1932, the 34-year old Amelia Earhart became the first woman to fly solo across the Atlantic. She went on to set other aviation records and is often quoted, or rather, misquoted, as having said, "Decide ... whether or not the goal is worth the risks involved. If it is, stop worrying." That's an incomplete quote designed to encourage you against worrying, which isn't too bad an idea in and of itself. However, Earhart's complete statement adds a different element. She said in full, "The time to worry is three months before a flight. Decide then whether or not the goal is worth the risks involved. If it is, stop worrying. To worry is to add another hazard. It retards reactions, makes one unfit. Hamlet would have been a bad aviator. He worried too much."

Earhart is not pointing out that one should never worry, but that there is a time for it and that the time for it is in advance of taking on the venture. The nature of the worry is in deciding if the achievement outweighs the risks to accomplish it. Once you've worried through that conundrum, once the decision is made to go ahead, then at that point quit worrying and get on with it. Decision made. Go for it!

"Is it worth it?" That's Earhart's question. And if you answer a well-considered "yes," then you've considered the gain you will receive from aiming for your goal, and you've counted the cost and looked at the risks. Think about the meaning of the word "worth." It connotes both value and cost. If you deem your venture "worth it," then you have decided in your heart that the value of gaining the prize outweighs the cost it may take in the attempt to obtain it. The attempt, even if you end up failing, is worth the risk in order to gain the prize.

IF AT FIRST...

And if at first you don't succeed ... emphasize the "at first" part, not the "don't succeed" part. Consider your attempt to be an "at first" in the series of steps it will take to finally arrive at your destination.

Too many people will fail at a relationship and give up on having another. Or a business attempt that goes haywire causes the entrepreneur to turn away from giving it another shot. Some will be turned back from their first major summit attempt because of sickness, injury, weather or fear and decide not to tackle the heights again.

Some will give up and not try again. But don't let that be you! If it really was worth it, move on from your "at first" try to your second try, and to your third try. The only reason not to try might be because you reevaluate the worth of the prize and feel the cost is too great. On rare occasions, I believe that could be the case.

But I encourage you to look deeply inside. Be honest with yourself: why would you not try again? Please do not excuse yourself from trying again by saying it isn't worth it if the truth is that you are just afraid. If you can see that your excuse is a cover for your fear, then admit the fear ... it's certainly OK to feel fear when faced with obstacles or hardships or dangers. People who have accomplished great and marvelous things are not without fear.

Before Amelia Earhart set out on her venture to fly around the world, she said she had faced the possibility of not making it back. But after she considered it, faced it, and decided to go ahead, she said there was no longer a reason to refer back to it. Earhart knew the risk, calculated the risk, accepted the risk, and did not look back.

DECIDE TO TAKE ACTION

The fear is not what's important in the end. The fear is not your challenge. *Facing* fear is the challenge. It's an attitude, a matter of counting the cost, recognizing the risk, accounting for assets, examining your experience. Having done that, put your face into the wind and feel its force. Lift your face into the rain and let the drops run down your cheeks. Set your face like a flint toward the unknown. There's a reason it's called "face your fears" ... turn your face toward them, move toward them, understand the difference between a lion in the streets and the *fear* of the lion in the streets.

It's not that feeling fear isn't real. The feeling is real ... but only as a feeling, an emotion. If your objective requires that you keep your feet moving, then don't let that fear paralyze you. Never allow fear alone to stop you. Keep moving! If you're afraid because you don't know enough, then read a book! If you're afraid because someone might let you down, it may be because you're using them to bolster you up ... stand on your own two feet! If you're afraid because of what people might think of you if you don't measure up, then get your own yardstick! Just do not let fear itself ever stop you from trying again.

Earhart said that deciding to take action is what's really hard ... after that, it's just a matter of sticking to it. Fears make a lot of noise sometimes, but that's all they are. If you decide to do something, you can do it, as Earhart said. Take action—the reward is the process itself.

SECOND CHANCE

Toward the end of my senior year in high school, my former neighbor sent word that he would take several of my mountaineering peers and myself up Mount Rainier at the end of May, which is early in the climbing season. Indeed, there was still ten feet of snow at Paradise, the most popular tourist spot on the mountain. At five thousand feet above sea level and right at timberline, Paradise sported a large overnight lodge, a tourist day lodge and museum and, at that time, a small ski run. This is where we climbed from and our route took us up to Panorama Point, then ascended several snowfields until we arrived at Camp Muir at ten thousand feet where we would spend the night.

Camp Muir is nestled in a saddle of snow and rock overlooking the Muir snowfields to the south and the Cowlitz Glacier to the north. There are three stone huts: one built for the professional guide service, another for park rangers, and a third for the general public which includes plywood bunks for the first twenty-five climbers who arrive. Other climbers set up camp in mountain tents.

Climbers get up after a few hours' sleep, clambering out of sleeping bags sometime between midnight and two in the morning, so that they can be on the glaciers of the upper slopes while snow is still frozen hard across crevasses. Starting too late means descending from the summit after the warmer afternoon has softened the snow, making the climbers vulnerable to breaking through and falling into a crevasse. Even though climbers always rope together when climbing on a glacier, a fall means that the other climbers on the rope team must go into action to stop the falling climber as the rope goes taut. So, climbers start very early in the morning.

RISK

One climbing party had reached the summit early in the week and they were the first team to reach the summit that year. Of the four groups heading for the summit this Saturday morning, we were the first on the slopes, our three rope teams working by flashlight along the ridge leading up from Muir toward Gibraltar. Gibraltar is a large outcropping of volcanic rock that rises about a thousand feet on the southeast side of Rainier to a snow covered top at 12,700 feet.

We crossed a rocky ledge that varied between four to ten feet wide. The ledge took about an hour for us to cross, and the sun had just come up as we began the traverse. Above us, impressively huge icicles hung menacingly, some of them ten feet or longer, looking like a trap in an Indiana Jones movie ... make a wrong move and find yourself skewered from head to toe! Fortunately, none of us stepped on a trigger, and we all worked our way across the rock. If I thought the exposure here was serious—a fall would have carried you a thousand feet down—the next section was a steep ascent up the left side of Gibraltar, a four-hundred foot, icy snow chute that led the last half of the way to the top of Gibraltar. A slip here would be difficult to stop, and it would have been a speedy, and probably fatal, descent to the base of the glacier below. There was nothing but the steep slope, blue sky, and that icy chute extending all the way down the mountain. This was the scariest part of the climb for me.

Once committed to the slope, there was only one thing to do— follow the snow chute up, crampons attached to climbing boots for gripping ice and hard snow, maintaining balance and not looking down. Actually, I think I did look down ... I wanted to come back home having sensed the full effect of the climb ... but I did not look for long! An hour or so working up the snow chute brought us to a wonderful resting spot on top of Gibraltar where several climbers who had set up a camp the day before were preparing themselves for the climb to the summit.

There was wind, although the weather was mostly sunny with a slight haze in the vastness of the air pounding the mountain. Those in the know said the winds were running up to sixty miles an hour. I had a movie camera with me and at a point about half way between Gibraltar and the summit, a gust hit us hard enough to knock me over as I was filming. Even though the wind was strong, there was exhilaration about it as if the mountain wanted to make sure we meant business if we were going to conquer its altitudinous slopes, and we did mean business.

Climbing above ten or twelve thousand feet means for the average climber that breathing becomes more labored. Along with the others on my rope team, I did what is called rest stepping. A step is taken up, your weight remains on your back leg, and you take an extra breath or two, both for the extra oxygen and to rest the leg. Another step is taken, the other leg rests, you take another extra breath or two … and so on to the summit.

Altitude sickness is fairly common and if it hits you, it often happens around the ten thousand or the fourteen thousand foot level. One of our climbers, a high school buddy of mine, got sick just four hundred feet below the rim of the summit crater. He could not continue, so one of the experienced climbers stayed with him as the rest of the party continued upward.

Because our climb was so early in the climbing season, only one crevasse was visibly open and required a detour around it. Otherwise, the upper slopes are mainly a matter of putting one foot in front of the other and rest stepping all the way. At around ten in the morning, we crested the summit crater. The crater is a slight, snow filled, concave dip about a quarter mile across. From where we reached the crater on the south side, we looked across to Columbia Crest, the true summit and highest point on the mountain. We crossed the quarter-mile crater quickly and, upon reaching the spot where there was not one inch higher to climb in the entire State of Washington, we dropped our backpacks, drank some water from our water bottles, and dug out the metal tube that contained the summit register where those who made the summit could record their accomplishment with a date and signature.

I took more film of us. It isn't dramatic—mostly everyone just sat or stretched out, resting from the strenuous climb. I thought maybe someone would wave a flag or something, but I had to settle for a couple of fellow climbers half heartedly waving their hand at the camera. We stayed for about a half hour, the second team on top of the mountain that year.

The descent was fast and, rather than risk that icy chute again and the ledges and icicles of the face of Gibraltar, we descended, still roped, down the Ingraham Glacier and crossed the Cowlitz Glacier back to Camp Muir. There we again rested a bit, then packed up the overnight items we had not carried to the summit, and headed down the Muir snow fields to Paradise, arriving late in the afternoon. An adventure, a dream finally come true, the mountain I'd seen from my paper route now conquered, and I would be home for dinner to tell the story.

What if you accept the risk and fail? That is the nature of risk. You may not be winning everything you're attempting, but you're still in the arena, among those brave souls who know both victory and defeat, and you will know in the end the triumph of high achievement.

Logbook

FUMES *and a* PRAYER

CHAPTER NINE

OPPORTUNITY

op·por·tu·ni·ty noun \,ä-pər-ˈtü-nə-tē\

Latin opportunus: "favorable"
from ob portum veniens:
"coming toward a port"

English: "your ship just came in"

FUMES *and a* PRAYER

OPPORTUNITY

You can see the crowd, stirring up dust at the starting line. Bets are being taken—all are in favor of the confident and speedy hare. A pair of tortoise toes takes the white-chalked line, followed by the revved-up hare. At one side, the official raises his hand high in the air as the starting gun signals the start of the race.

The hare, bolting from the line is, within seconds, out of sight over the first hill. At the same time, you see the back feet of the tortoise shuffle toward the starting line.

Eventually, news reports flash to the crowd that the hare, so far ahead of his competition, has taken a detour to granny hare's house for some cookies and tea. Having eaten, drunk and relaxed, the hare decides he has plenty of time to catch a quick snooze in granny hare's hammock.

The day wears on. You check your watch. The hare should have crossed the distant finish line hours ago, but there are no reports … until suddenly the news desk jolts the crowd with the astonishing news that the tortoise is in sight and, in fact, only minutes from crossing the finish line.

Miles back, the hare awakens, groggy from a long afternoon nap, taking a few moments to remember where he is. Then with a start he remembers the race, shakes off the stiffness, stretches and sets off to finish the contest. But as he races around the last turn, the tortoise's nose crosses the finish line and the competition is over. Today the trophy still sits on the tortoise's mantle.

You have heard the usual moral: The race is not to the swift, but to the slow and steady. But that is not the real lesson of the fable. Think about it. The hare, after all, really *is* faster! The only reason the tortoise won was not that he tried harder, not because he was faster, not because he had more desire ... the tortoise won only because the hare stopped and took a nap! The tortoise did not win because he was slow and steady. He won only because the hare slept during the contest and he himself did not.

The *real* lesson of the fable is this: In competition, you cannot sleep ... your competitor isn't!

The tortoise simply took advantage of an opportunity—in this case, the competition napping—and, very importantly, was in the right place at the right time. This was not an accident. Neither was it serendipity, nor luck, nor the law of attraction. He was on the right road on the right day—on purpose. The tortoise could have been on the right road on the right day, and if the hare had not napped, the tortoise would have lost the race. But opportunity sailed in that day, and the tortoise was prepared to receive it.

When Your Ship Comes In

Isn't that true of any venture? When your ship comes in, it's best to be at the dock. If you don't know if your ship's coming in, but it might ... it's best to be at the dock. And if there's even a remote possibility that a ship might come in ... it's best to be at the dock. It won't matter if a whole fleet of ships come in, all at the same time, all laden with opportunity ... if you're not at the dock when all that opportunity shows up, your fortunes will never improve. The sad bumper sticker puts it aptly, "When my ship comes in, I'll probably be at the airport." If you want your ship to come in ... it's a good idea to be at the dock.

Look at this from the hare's perspective. Opportunity is not something you find when you are sleeping. Even if you are ahead in the race, even if your market position is currently number one, even if you outnumber the opposition, if you sleep through the time when your competition isn't, you are in danger of losing the race for your objective. You cannot cross the finish line in first place if you miss the opportunities when they are available to you.

WHEN YOU ARE ON THE SHIP

The word "opportunity"—"to port approaching," from Latin *ob portum veniens*—refers to the olden days of sailing when a ship took advantage of winds that were favorable to take the ship to its destination. Generally, modern sailboats are able to sail almost directly into the wind, a position called "close hauled," which means hauling the sailboat close to the direction the wind is coming from, like an airplane with a headwind. In olden days, without modern sail design and control and without the precision of today's keels to convert the sideways push of the wind into forward motion for the sailboat, a sailing vessel was much more at the mercy of the wind's direction than is true of most of today's sailboats. Ancient sailboats pretty much had to go in the direction the wind was blowing, so it was a good thing for a boat's skipper, if he wanted to come into a port, when the wind was blowing toward that port. A following or rear-quarter wind gave the skipper the opportunity to sail into port, and he might have had to wait a bit for the opportunity. But when it came, he'd better not have been sleeping.

Opportunity is not something you dream up or create, although you might create an environment where you remove limits and restrictions and thereby increase the chances for opportunity to sail in—you might build a dock, for instance. If you want to sail into port, you will have a better chance if you are aimed at, and within landing distance, of that port, and if you have your crew and equipment ready ... and if you stay awake, so when the wind blows you are in the right place at the right time.

GET IT WHILE THE GETTIN' IS GOOD

Because Yeager had evaded the Germans and escaped back to England, he had his choice of assignments back in the States. Several weeks before the end of World War II, Yeager chose Wright Field at Dayton, Ohio, for his next military assignment, a choice based on only one factor: his wife Glennis was pregnant and sick, and Wright Field was the closest base to his hometown of Hamlin, West Virginia, where she could get help from his mother.

Wright Field is where Yeager's ship came in. He was at the right place at the right time, as we saw in chapter seven. With all the airplane time soon to be available to him at Wright, if Yeager had gone to another air base instead, we would not know his name today as the first man to break the sound barrier. I suppose we could say in Yeager's case that his ship *did* come in at the airport.

The important thing about Yeager's career is that when he saw the opportunity right there where he was at Wright Field, he took advantage of it. Picture someone at the dock. Their ship comes in, loaded with opportunity, and instead of unloading the ship they decide to go see what's at the other docks. How foolish! When opportunity shows up, get to work. Get all of it you can while it's available! Don't slack. Don't stop. Don't sleep.

WHILE THEY WERE SLEEPING

There is a remarkable story in ancient scripture. In this case, "sleeping while your competition isn't" proved deadly in battle. Sometime around the twelfth century BC the Midianites, who were descendants of Abraham's fourth son, Midian, were camped against the Israelites, who were descendants of Abraham's second son, Isaac. This was no small vanguard; the Midianite army numbered around 135,000, nearly three times the entire US Continental Army in 1776, and over five times as many as the soldiers, airmen and civilians at Joint Base Lewis-McChord (combined Fort Lewis/McChord Air Force Base, in 2010) near where I live. That's a lot of Midianites … enough to make an entire military corps today.

The situation was beyond grim for the Israelites. For seven years the Midianites had the upper hand and used that upper hand to decimate the crops throughout the nation and to destroy their farm animals. In an agrarian society, dependent upon their farms and animals, the oppression was extreme. The Israelites were so overwhelmed by the Midianites that they were forced to flee their villages and farms and live in caves and in the mountains to save themselves. They had nothing left to eat. The economy was destroyed.

The Midianites were possibly the first to domesticate camels. They had so many of them that they couldn't be counted, and even in the military encampment in this story, it's said their camels were as innumerable as the sand on a beach. They came to waste the land of the Israelites yet again, and they meant deadly business.

A wheat farmer's son named Gideon was called on to lead an army against the Midianites. In something of an underground resistance, Gideon was threshing wheat in a wine vat to keep it hidden from the Midianites. Though perhaps for different reasons, Gideon's response to the call was similar to George Washington's when in 1775 Washington was called upon by the Continental Congress to lead the Continental Army. Washington said, "With the utmost sincerity, I do not think myself equal to the Command I am honored with." Gideon felt the same way ... not up to it.

To begin with, the story indicates Gideon was afraid. I can't blame him—his army numbered only 32,000. He's outnumbered more than four to one! Can you imagine a football game where one side has eleven men on the field while the other team fields forty-six? Those were Gideon's odds in the beginning.

Because there was a spiritual element to the events, Gideon was instructed to do the unthinkable—reduce his army! So an announcement was given, a very practical option from the outnumbered soldiers' perspective. Those who were afraid, shaking in their boots, were allowed to turn around and go home. While you might expect an army whose people are devastated by a foreign entity to rally in a patriotic display of arms, over two-thirds of Gideon's army leaves. If the odds were tough to begin with, they are now ridiculous. Ten thousand soldiers remained. Now the odds are thirteen and a half to one. That eleven-man football squad on the field now faces, on the other side of the line of scrimmage, a hundred and forty-eight opponents.

OPPORTUNITY

Now Gideon really has something to worry about. Yet he is called upon to exercise a great amount of faith. He is told yet again to reduce his force. To implement the reduction, a very practical field test is given to the men. The ten thousand remaining soldiers are taken to a river where they may drink. Plastic water bottles had not been invented yet, and the men gathered to drink directly from the water in the river.

Try to picture this: if the average adult male's shoulder width is about eighteen inches, and if the men lined up side by side, shoulder-to-shoulder, then the soldiers stretched out along the river bank for over two and a half miles. Perhaps they lined up and took turns; but however it was done, it took a good deal more than a few minutes to observe how the men drank.

The deciding factor was this. If a man got down on his hands and knees, put his face to the water and lapped it up like a dog, he was to be sent home. (I've never seen anybody drink that way, but maybe it was stylish in the day.) But if he knelt on a knee and scooped the water into his hand, he was to stay.

I'm sure the reason for this was to find out which soldiers were constantly alert. Someone down on all fours lapping water like a dog is vulnerable in a surprise attack. The soldier who is on a knee but upright, drinking water from his hand, is able both to keep his eyes open to his surroundings and to keep the other hand on his weapon, just in case. Those vigilant fighters are the ones you want on your team.

Gideon's team gets cut to just three hundred men—men smart enough to be ready on an instant's notice to respond to a military attack. The odds now, though, are an astonishing four hundred fifty to one. On the football field, our eleven-man team now has to move the ball against an opponent with nearly five thousand players on the field. That's beyond incredible! The words "mission: impossible" come to mind.

The tortoise's chances of winning the race against the hare were about the same. Impossible! How can you race at two-tenths of a mile an hour against a hare with a speed of forty-five miles an hour (assuming our hare is the European Brown Hare)? The hare runs two hundred forty-five times faster than the tortoise! There's only one way to win this.

BAUER'S BASICS OF BATTLE

Perhaps Gideon knew an early version of the story of the tortoise's race against the hare. He does come up with an ingenious plan that begins with an attack in the middle of the night. He knows the enemy troops are camped together in one place ... sleeping. And he knows the odds.

Many have tried to summarize the basics of military strategy. The Chinese general Sun Tzu defined thirteen of them in *The Art of War*. Napoleon listed one hundred fifteen principles of war. Nathaniel Bedford Forest, American general during the Civil War, had just one: "get there first with the most men." The *United States Army Field Manual* lists nine.

I am not a military strategist, and my tendency is to think through complicated material in order to boil it down to basics that I can understand and that I can explain to others ... so that we all get it and remember it. So you understand that the following ideas can be expanded, explained and extended. With that disclaimer, here are Bauer's Basics of Battle. There are three of them.

OPPORTUNITY

Bauer's Basics of Battle, whether for an army or for a business or for a football team, are:

- Intelligence
- Surprise
- Maneuverability.

The basic tactical approach is to take advantage of your own strengths and to exploit the enemy's weaknesses by finding out everything you can about the other side, hit them in a way they are not expecting, and stay flexible and moveable during an attack.

It's pretty dumb to let your enemy know what you're about to do. Ever see a football team go into the huddle? They gather shoulder pad to shoulder pad, scrunch over a bit, hide the play call from the other team and try to trick the other team into thinking they're not about to do something they actually are about to do. Coaches cover their mouths with a clipboard or play sheet when calling in plays, in case the other team has someone who can read lips.

At the same time, it's a great idea to find out everything you can about your opponent's plans. Before game day, the football team studies film from their opponent's previous games. On the field, they watch to see which players take the field before any given play.

Maneuverability is enhanced as soon as the ball is hiked as huge linemen push to open a hole so the ball carrier can maneuver his way up field toward the goal. The ball carrier who cuts quickly around defenders succeeds in making progress through defensive lines, past defensive players and ultimately to the goal line.

For Gideon, his enemy had a lot of strengths—numbers, weapons, mobility and a winning streak. But his enemy's weakness was over-confidence. The Midianite army was huge and had always been successful because of their size. From the Midianites' perspective, a successful attack against them was inconceivable. They were blinded by their own strength, thinking logically to a wrong conclusion.

When Gideon approached the enemy line, he did it at night. With an aide, he snuck to a Midianite outpost to gather intelligence. He overheard two Midianites; one told the other about a disturbing dream where a loaf of bread rolled into their camp and crushed one of their tents. The other man understood the dream to mean that their defeat at the sword of Gideon was imminent.

In the middle of the night, Gideon wakes his band of three hundred men. He divides them into three groups of one hundred men each, and instructs them to carry a trumpet, a torch and a jar in which to hide the torch. They take positions around the Midianite camp. At Gideon's signal they break the jars, raise their lamps, make a terrific racket with the horns and shout like crazy. Surprise! The Midianites, frightened and confused so badly that when they grab their swords in the black darkness and noisy confusion, they swing their swords wildly, massacring their own army! Thousands of enemy troops died right there. In the chase that followed, Gideon's army captured and defeated the enemy. His people enjoyed peace and protection, their land, crops and herds now safe.

Opportunity Doesn't Knock

Gideon took advantage of Opportunity. He was as small to his enemy as a tortoise is slow to a hare. The Midianites slept. The hare slept. The opportunity for both Gideon and the hare to take advantage of a sleeping opponent presented a chance to win because they themselves were available, awake, alert, and active.

Opportunity doesn't knock. Most often it comes your way without fanfare ... no parade, no trumpets, no pageantry. When the ancient crew was anchored off shore, no one fired off cannons to announce an approaching wind. A favorable shift in wind happened in real time and somebody needed to be watchful of the wind indicator, perhaps a pennant, perhaps the pattern on the surface of the water, in order to make the call for all hands on deck.

Two Lessons from the Hare and the Tortoise

The first lesson of the Hare and the Tortoise is from the Hare's perspective: don't go to sleep in competition ... your enemy isn't. There's a second lesson from the story. When you think about the attitude it would take for the hare to stop and take a nap in the middle of the race, two things should come to mind. First is the arrogance of the hare, the assumption that he was so much better than the tortoise that no matter what, he could and would outrace the tortoise. It does, after all, seem like a logical conclusion—logical, but wrong. He's faster ... he should win. His arrogance gives him a natural confidence, so natural that he feels he doesn't even have to monitor the tortoise's presumed slowness. He's ahead, after all, leading the pack of two racers in the competition. Of course, he will win. All bets are on him!

The other realization that should come to mind is that the tortoise, naturally slow, has only one chance to win ... if the hare stops running. If the hare sustained an injury, committed a foul and was ejected by the umpire, became dehydrated or ran out of energy and fainted, if something happened to the hare, then there's a chance, a slim possibility of hope, of winning the race. The tortoise might be smaller, slower, shyer—but he can eventually stand in the winner's circle, victorious, trophy in hand, if he doesn't quit out of fear that he's under-resourced or under-manned in comparison to his competition. Opportunity is like that. You seldom see it coming. But when it shows up, it's the one who's not sleeping that can claim it.

If you are currently doing well, in first place perhaps, you still must keep your eyes open, and never assume that your competition isn't going to see an opportunity that's not available to you. In other words, don't let the ease of your current popularity or the comforts of your current position lull you into slumber.

If you're the underdog, your only hope may be in an as yet unforeseen opportunity. The idea you haven't seen yet, the resource you haven't picked up yet, the asset you haven't obtained yet, the client you're not aware of today, may be just around the next corner. You never know.

That is, you never know unless you go around the next corner. If you stop here and now—and this may happen simply because, since you don't know, you have no hope or enthusiasm or confidence—but if you stop, you will *never* know. You never know what a day will bring. Perhaps tomorrow, perhaps next month, perhaps next quarter … perhaps today. Perhaps it *will* be around the next corner. You don't know, so you keep going with the knowledge that opportunities do exist, and yours may be around that corner.

"Be Prepared" is the Boy Scout's motto. Robert Baden-Powell, the founder of the Boy Scouts in 1907, was asked once, "Be prepared for what?" Baden-Powell replied, "Why, for any old thing!" Exactly! That's the nature of both risk and opportunity. For risk—be well equipped, be trained and be courageous. For opportunity—be awake and get to the dock.

One thing you do know: if you stop now and don't go around the next corner, whatever opportunity you might have had will never be yours to take advantage of.

WIN SOME, LOSE SOME...

YOUR GREATEST OPPORTUNITY FOR IMPROVING

Consider this. Being in first place might not be the best place for you. Have you ever set the bar high, then trained, travailed and nearly triumphed … but you came up just short of the treasured trophy? What do you do when your best efforts don't get you to the top?

What if I told you that reaching the top is not necessarily the best condition for improvement? Why not be in first place? The answer may surprise you.

If you sit with me at the table in the hotel conference room, you will not notice the butterflies, but they are there. The smell of the steak dinner still lingers and the chatter of a hundred attendees fills the air. The district winners of the Toastmasters International Inspirational Speech Competition are about to be announced. I am one of the competitors, and going to the World Championship of Public Speaking contest in California is at stake.

The speech has to be within five to seven minutes. Months earlier, my first, rough draft delivery was over nine minutes! I slaved for days to cut and pare the speech to be under seven minutes so I wouldn't be disqualified at this competition.

My local Toastmasters club advanced me to the Area Competition where I took first place. To get really good I gave my speech 15 times at 10 clubs for practice and for evaluation. Every time I gave the speech, feedback from listeners helped me improve. That led to taking first place at the Division Contest, and I knew I was on my way with a winning speech. I'd passed the first three levels of competition with flying colors. I was #1.

Now the big event ... the District competition, just two steps away from the World Championships! I know I have a winning speech. I feel like an Olympic athlete ... I've certainly trained hard enough! Of the seven competitors, I speak first. I know that's not a great position, because like figure skating competitions, judges sometimes leave room in scoring the first competitor in case a better competitor follows—but I corral all my confidence and take the stage.

I take a moment to scan the audience. My first words are solid and projected to the entire audience of about a hundred people. The mind map I've stored in my memory is clear and I follow it well. My voice is strong, the audience laughs at the appropriate points, their heads nod in understanding and empathy as I unfold my story and then conclude with a memorable challenge and pithy takeaway. The audience applauds loudly and encouragingly as I step down from the platform, escape to the hallway and find my way back to my seat as the competition judges fill in their score sheets.

The competition continues through the other speakers. The competition is stiff!

When all is literally said and done, the competition chairperson takes the platform, certificates and trophies in hand. Announcing winners would start with third place, and the third place winner was ... *not* me! Relief and tension joined the butterflies. A mental drumroll beat through my brain. "Our second place winner is ...." The wait to hear which of the other competitors would be in second place was intense. ".... is .... Dennis Bauer."

What? Not first? Not going to California? I planted a gracious smile on my face and went forward to accept my second place trophy. You competitors know exactly the combination of disappointment at not winning, appreciation for placing at all, and grace to accept the results.

All the hard work, the hours and hours of preparation, the miles and miles driven to give practice speeches, the many drafts and revisions ... all in that final moment come down to second place, not first.

How about you? Ever worked hard on something very important to you? You gave it your very best shot ... yet you came in second?

SECOND-PLACE WINNER

In 1946 a former Army-Air Corp pilot, tired of landing at airports and finding no ground transportation, bought three cars, and with a spot at the Willows Run Airport near Detroit, began the first car rental company located at airports. His name was Warren Avis and the company was the Avis Airlines Rent-A-Car System. His big idea was to build a company that provided car rental services at airports.

Avis became the world's largest car rental company in the country. Competition grew however, and eventually Hertz took the number one spot. In 1962 Avis began its famous "We're #2 ... we try harder" ad campaign. That ad propelled Avis into the #1 spot in the airport car rental business, and the slogan is still used today.

When I got the #2 spot in the speech competition, I recalled the Avis slogan. You can understand that being in first place is fun and filled with limelight. But being in second place is more motivating and more challenging. Being in second place means that I must try harder. The end result of trying harder is even greater improvement in the skills of preparation, organization, content and delivery.

Who has greater motivation to improve ... the one in first place, or the one in second place? Avis has it right. Being in second place is where you spend extra effort, where you do more research, where you try new methods. Being in first place is rewarding ... being in second place is challenging. The end result is intense motivation to change, to grow and to innovate.

When you are anywhere behind first place, what do you do? To make any progress at all requires the three major fundamentals that apply to every business: Aviate, Navigate, Communicate.

First, you must understand the basic elements of your endeavor. What is the core process or product of your business? Rather than a fuzzy, generalized vision statement, it must be specific, definite, definable. The core of my speaking and writing business is: I get my point across to an audience. If I don't do that, I have no business. Everything else is built on that. What is at the core of your business? This is what you must focus on every day and in every business decision you make ... the basics. Write it out.

Second, you must have a very clear picture of where you are, where you want to go, and the steps you need to take to get there. Putting your navigational plan on paper makes it harder to get off course and, at the same time easier to make those small course corrections that are always necessary on any journey. Write it down.

OPPORTUNITY

1) Where are you? What assets and resources do you have available at this moment? What is your current market, sales figures, budget and cash flow?

2) Where do you want to be one year from now and five years from now? What will it look like if you could take a picture of it?

3) What steps do you need to take to get from here to there, to bridge the gap from where you are to where you want to go? Write it out.

Third, talk to someone outside your business, someone not emotionally involved in your venture. Share the core of your business, where you are right now, where you want to end up, and the steps you're taking to get there. A good consultant gives you feedback—help with direction and destination, competition, course correction, and conditions you need to know about. The consultant brings clarity, insight and reality into your efforts.

I challenge you to consider the benefit of being in second place, the advantage of not having quite reached the bar you set for yourself. Write out the three fundamental aspects of advancing your venture. Take another run at it, keep learning, become stronger, advance farther … and you will be the one who constantly improves. You may be #2 now, but you try harder!

The world of opportunity works for you when you are available, awake, alert, and active.

FUMES *and a* PRAYER

OPPORTUNITY

Logbook

FUMES *and a* PRAYER

CHAPTER TEN

CONCLUSION

con·clu·sion *noun* \kən-ˈklü-zhən\

the last part of the story

FUMES *and a* PRAYER

CONCLUSION

In the next few minutes, with the help of a skilled air traffic controller, I flew down nearly to the beginning of the runway, and I could see clearly. I landed smoothly on Runway Two-Six-Right.

I taxied off the runway toward the refueling area and passed in front of some of those big brother jets from the sky looking down over their noses at my little airplane.

At the fuel pump, I topped off both tanks and figured I'd had about fifteen minutes left of fumes and a prayer.

My passengers knew it was not a pretty landing. But we walked away from it, and we would fly again. As a friend and passenger told me one time after a gust caused a bouncy landing, "Any landing you walk away from is a good landing!"

HOME FOR DINNER

As the plates of spaghetti were served to each of us at the dinner table, the conversation with my three kids revolved around the activities of the day—their math, reading and other schoolwork; their play at the park across the street; their hopes for TV that evening. I arrived home from work at Boeing a little before dinner, and now I began my usual dinnertime presentation with, "There I was...." My kids knew a story was about to follow, and I tried every day to have something interesting to share with them from my day.

The daily "There I was..." stories mostly revolved around a challenge I'd faced that day ... sometimes funny (at least I tried to make it so), often trivial, but mostly related to something to overcome. Topics ranged from: The driver who cut me off in the commute that morning and how I felt about it after the near miss with the car next to me—to the newly implemented mechanical unit I was given to install in the belly of the airplane, only to find that another assembly was already in that same spot and what I said to the liaison engineer who came to figure out a fix. One night the story was why my scalp was glued together after I'd split it open on a fin-shaped antennae fastened underneath the plane, which I bumped into that day.

In retrospect, each "There I was..." had something at its core that was unexpected. I hadn't expected to be cut off on the freeway, I hadn't expected another assembly to be where mine was to be installed, and I hadn't expected to be injured that day. If the story was about a past event—driving in a blizzard in Colorado, taking a college midterm the first time I took a prescribed Valium for a tight back muscle, jumping like a frog to catch a rope over water on the obstacle course at basic training—the story always had at its core an

212

CONCLUSION

unexpected obstacle to overcome, a hurdle to get over, a crisis to resolve.

These were the themes of my dinner table stories. Whatever the story's scale, reliving the episode at the table with a plate of spaghetti and three attentive pairs of eyes and ears was the perfect culmination of my adventure.

PERSONAL JOURNAL

Scene:

It is Spring. I sip my white chocolate mocha at the outdoor table at Starbucks, my mind in a muddle.

Backstory:

In the space of twelve short months I faced three major obstacles that threatened to put me into a tailspin. In marriage, in business and in personal finances I faced major difficulties.

Action:

I place my personal journal on the glass-top table, open it to a new page, uncap my favorite gel pen and write one word at the top of the page: "AVIATE."

Under that word, I write out those elements of life that seem most basic to me at that time. Serious about the exercise, I look beyond the Starbucks umbrella for several moments, trying to clear my head. At times like this it's easy to get lost in a fog of thoughts and confusions. Under "AVIATE," the black ink flows as I write:

1. Get control of basics:
  - Eat right.
    - Get back on weight loss program
    - Eat no more than one helping
    - Limit sugars
      - Drink water, not soda
      - One dessert/day. Just one!
    - Eat regularly through the day
    - Do not eat late in the day
    - Eat good stuff—veggies, fiber, fruit, etc.
  - Sleeping.
    - Try to get eight hours/night, seven minimum
    - That's sleep time, reading is extra
  - Exercise.
    - Walk/jog 5x wk—30 minutes minimum
    - Weights 3x wk—follow routine
  - Quiet Time.
    - Record in journal what I read, ideas, prayers

Eating, sleeping and exercise … pretty basic stuff. I'm guessing that's why they're called "basics." I figure that these three things are pretty much the equivalent of keeping an airplane under control. First things first, so if I never make any progress out of the fog and if I never talk to anyone about my problems, at least I'll still be in control of my day-to-day life.

I turn the page. At the top of the next page I write a second word: "NAVIGATE." I take a sip of my mocha in another thinking break. Under "NAVIGATE" I divide the page into three sections. In the first section I write out where I am. I list all the current assets and resources I have available to me at this moment. Here are some of my notes I write:

1. Take stock of where I am (what do I have?):
    1) Without a home of my own
        - House going up for sale, it's in pre-foreclosure
        - I do have a roof over my head
    2) No regular income
        - $ from teaching, $385 from school district
        - business acc't empty, personal acc't overdrawn
        - $12 and change in my pocket
    3) Car is running well
    4) Office furniture and video equipment I can sell
    5) I have a following; get them into coaching, workshops
    6) I have rough plans for StoryTelling 101 Workshops
    7) I have people who help me:
        - Toastmasters clubs, networks, coach, friends
    8) I have a sound mind, and I'm not panicked

In the next section I write out a verbal snapshot of what it will look like when I get to where I want to be:
2. Where do I want to be?
    1) Financially sound
        - Regular income
        - Debts paid off
        - Growing bank account
        - Investments—finally live off of investments
        - Benevolent giving
    2) Speaking regularly as keynote speaker
    3) Coaching speakers one-on-one

4) Workshops for speech craft and StoryTelling 101

5) Books published and selling

6) A home of my own

7) Systems in place for business

    - Marketing and sales

    - Product and fulfillment

8) Driving a 2-seat convertible roadster, a Pontiac Solstice

9) Enjoying a great relationship with my kids

10) Fit and healthy

The last section under "NAVIGATE" fills in the blank between where I am now and where I want to be when it's all over. I write out twenty-one steps that seem essential for the journey. Understand that this is my list, a series of steps I want to follow to get me to where I want to go. You should have a list of steps also, and I imagine yours will be quite different. Here's a partial list of mine. (Some steps are personal and not included here.)

3. How to get there:

    1) Sell house, if it's not rescued

    2) Sub teach as much as possible for working capital

    3) Compete in speech contests for experience, credibility

    5) Design, schedule, market StoryTelling 101 Workshops

    6) Write book #1, publish and market

    8) Make schedule to pay off debts

    9) Give 10%

    10) Take Dave Ramsey personal finance course

    11) Find apartment or house to rent

    12) Design ongoing marketing system

    14) Save 10%

    17) Journal every day

18) Read my Bible every day

20) Write magazine articles

21) Develop new habit: One thing at a time.
   No multi-tasking unless absolutely necessary!

The white chocolate mocha becomes lukewarm. At the top of the next page I write the third word: "COMMUNICATE." I write some notes here, but more importantly for this step, I meet with a Life Coach who knows where I am, with whom I share my destination and the steps I'm about to take to get there. Most importantly, as you know by now, the Life Coach is not involved emotionally, so is able to give me feedback on what I've written, to make suggestions and to give me feedback on my progress.

I stand up and leave. With my journal under my arm and the empty mocha cup tossed in the trash can, my step perks up. In writing it all down in my journal, I discovered mental clarity; I discovered a sense of direction; I discovered hope. It's an extremely important exercise when life hits you hard, head-on, when you feel like you've run out of gas and you're coasting on fumes and a prayer. Write it down.

Life Is a Day at a Time

The adventure over northern Colorado comes to an end. Everyone walks away. The next morning we all climb in the Cessna again and continue on to our destination in Indiana. Another day. Lessons are learned. Stories are told.

The adventure of life, however, isn't over. You and I are still walking through it. Just today I face The Unexpected. It isn't life-threatening, but it alters my plans by several hours as a family member needs help retrieving her pickup truck where she had a flat tire last night and no spare—two hours away.

I know the basics. Family needs come before business needs. I leave my writing and we get a new tire, drive nearly to Ocean Shores, change the tire, jump start the engine because the emergency flashers drained the battery, stop at McDonalds for chicken nuggets, and get home over six hours later. I wanted to write today.

But Opportunity shows up through The Unexpected—the chance to make a difference in someone's life, to care about someone other than myself. And besides, it's a gorgeous, cold winter day in the Pacific Northwest—a great day for a drive. It is indeed a great day.

I wonder what tomorrow will bring.

CONCLUSION

HOME FOR DINNER

Fumes and a prayer. Sometimes life is like that. You pray your way to a gas station. You get run down, or the things of life get you down. How you handle the situation right then will make the difference between success and failure, maybe even life or death. Take acceptable risks. Get all the experience you can. Learn from failures and move on. Be ready for opportunities. Then go home for dinner.

Aviate. Navigate. Communicate. I challenge you to memorize these three words—and in that order. When The Unexpected happens, and it will: Aviate, Navigate, Communicate. You will have a smooth landing that you walk away from, and you, my friend, will fly again.

FUMES *and a* PRAYER

Logbook

FUMES *and a* PRAYER

FOUNDATION

foun·da·tion *noun* \faün-'dā-shən\

the base upon which one stands;
groundwork

FUMES *and a* PRAYER

Maybe it's from watching "Surviving the Cut" on Discovery Channel ... shows like US Air Force Pararescue school, where the course is so tough that only one in ten survive the cut; like Army Ranger school, where one out of three make it; Navy Explosive Ordnance school and Marine Recon school ... schools where toughness, will and grit show a guy what he's made of ... show a guy that he can go farther, do more and survive longer than he ever thought he could do. Limits are tested and expanded ... limits of endurance, of will power, of fatigue, of strength.

Maybe it's from watching other guys endure the rigors of these schools so that they can say they did it, that they finished ... that they can go on to do their part to protect and defend the rest of us who are content to watch them do it on TV. These stories move me. Seeing someone else take on extreme difficulty, not quit, make it to the end ... this inspires me.

Maybe you're like me when it comes to social media. I'm not one to use social media for promoting my political or religious views; I use Facebook for social and business purposes, for announcements of personal happenings and opportunities.

But I've been thinking. I do have a strong personal faith. Yesterday I had pictures going through my mind of these guys going through the military schools, and it made me think of how tough I am (or am not). And while I have not expressed it much on Facebook, I felt compelled to take my stand ... to make a statement here of the single impetus behind all my aims, activities and aspirations.

Years ago I put my faith in God, I became a Christian, I accepted the Bible as God's book, his revelation to us of truth, of our fallen and sinful condition, of redemption and reconciliation through accepting the sacrifice of his son, Jesus Christ who did what we could not do ... live a perfect, sinless life and offer himself on the cross as the sacrifice to pay for our sins, perfect and acceptable before God, on our behalf. I have not lived perfectly—but he did, and the day I saw that, I gave my life to him. I am a follower of Christ.

Those who know me very much at all know that I am far from perfect. I have done things that are disgraceful. Sometimes I've done things without meaning to ... more often I knew what I was doing, and did it anyway. I've hurt people; I've been a bad example and have not lived life the way you would expect a Christian to live. Where I'm aware of it, I ask forgiveness and turn away from what I was doing wrong. Mainly, I seem to keep asking God to give me wisdom to know what is right ... maybe because the older I get the grayer many things have become ... and I keep asking for strength to do what I sometimes don't want to do, or to keep from things I shouldn't do, but want to.

Yesterday, while working outside filling in a hole my dogs had dug under the fence—which I discovered after getting phone calls from kind people in the neighborhood who had found the rascally golden retrievers—an old hymn kept going through my mind. Actually it was just one line, which is typical of me ... I recall a line or two that keep replaying. The line was, "Am I a soldier of the cross, a follower of the Lamb..."

Maybe it's "Surviving the Cut," but I made a parallel in my mind to those soldiers slugging and slogging it out, sometimes losing

226

consciousness in swimming exercises, sometimes battling to get a
Zodiac raft through breakers and surf, sometimes carrying 200-pound
dummies in exhausted, numbed and shaking arms ... a parallel with
how much fight I put into my own daily life, a fight to overcome evil
with good, a fight not to entertain wrong thoughts, a fight to
discipline my body and my time.

> Am I a soldier of the cross,
> A follower of the Lamb,
> And shall I fear to own His cause,
> Or blush to speak His Name?

It's time for me to dust off a verse from the Psalms that a pastor
gave to me a long time ago. "Through God we shall do valiantly."
(Psalm 60:12 and Psalm 108:13) Being valiant means having
bravery, boldness and courage. Sometimes I have not lived well that
way. It's my heart's desire to do so, though, and seeing what men
endure on "Surviving the Cut" reminds me that I can do more than I
think I can do, that I can fight harder than I fight, that I can be more
disciplined than I am, that I can stand firm longer than I have before.
I am moved to better serve the God who loves me, who is amazingly
affectionate towards me, who is in fact crazy about me.

Because of Jesus Christ, my sins are cleansed, or, more
accurately I suppose, I am cleansed from my sins ... either way,
they're gone ... bye bye! The Bible says they are "removed as far as
the east is from the west" and that "He (God) remembers them no
more." I assume that the east/west thing is infinite. Before you and
the rest of the world, there's a lot about me to point your finger at ...
but that's no longer the case with God. He's not pointing fingers. My
name's on the record in heaven ... not because of anything I have

done, not because of the good I've tried to do or because of kindnesses toward others ... but only because of God's grace and mercy—words which I now treasure—my name is on the record ... I believed, and I was saved.

I am convinced that the current fads of "you've gotta follow your heart" and "the law of attraction" and "if you can visualize it, you can have it" have their limitations. Serious limitations. So much of it rings of narcissism. Following them has been bad for me. I remember the ancient scripture where God warns his people to "remember all the Lord's commands and obey them and not become unfaithful by following your own heart and your own eyes" (Numbers 15:39).

Those guys in the sand carrying the heavy Zodiac rafts, or in the pool swimming lap after lap underwater even to the point sometimes of unconsciousness, or carrying 100-pound rucksacks at 4 AM for miles, or crawling uphill with their faces in the mud while trainers yell at them and spray water from hoses into their mouths ... those guys learn to follow orders ... or they're dead.

I do not want to be "dead" in any sense at all. I'm too old now for military service, and not sure I'd have the heart to do what these guys do, though I deeply appreciate that they do it. But I do have a life to live out in the service of the kingdom of an indescribable God, a life to live for the creator of the universe, a life to live in service and obedience to the one who saved me, who put new clothes on me and who will one day call me home to an indescribable and eternal adventure.

There's no longer a "cut" that I have to make. That's good because I wouldn't have survived it ... and God's book explains why. Jesus pulled me out of the muck and mire and did what I could not do. At the same time, he's got me here to serve him, and sometimes that feels just like being in pararescue school. In that sense, I do hope to stick it out, to fight hard, to endure hardship like a good soldier, a soldier of the cross.

So, here I take my stand. In this final chapter you know my struggle, my savior, and my song. In speeches, I give mostly personal and business help based on what I learned in Aviate, Navigate and Communicate. But in this book, if you've read this far, you know where I'm coming from ... and where I'm headed.

Maybe you'll see me fail at times. Maybe you'll see my face all muddy. Maybe you'll see me get back up again. Maybe you'll see me take a hill or something. I'm sure you'll see me from time to time running on fumes and a prayer.

But one thing I know. If you too are a Christ-follower, you'll see my face at the finish line ... where I look forward to hearing Him say, "Well, done, good and faithful servant."

And I will be Home for dinner.

FUMES *and a* PRAYER

Logbook

ABOUT THE AUTHOR

Dennis Bauer is an author and award-winning speaker. He is also the founder and teacher of "StoryTelling 101 Workshops with Dennis Bauer," as well as a speaking coach. Dennis and his wife live in the Puget Sound area of Washington State where there are rain forests and deserts, forests and plains, inland salt water and fresh water, ocean beaches at sea level and mountains up to fourteen thousand feet.

Dennis is an alumnus of Colorado Christian University in Denver. He worked for Boeing, was a flight instructor and aircraft mechanic, was in the ministry, owned a video production company, owned a real estate company, and now enjoys sharing life-lessons with groups of all sizes.

Book Dennis Bauer to speak to your organization or at your next special event. Visit his website at www.DennisBauer.com or email him at Dennis@DennisBauer.com.

Made in the USA
Middletown, DE
13 September 2015